Editorial

At the end of February the novelist Sir Kazuo Ishiguro expressed concern about the 'climate of fear' that has beset many starting writers, inhibiting them from writing what and how they want. There are problems of theme, point of view, and even of form that might prove toxic to explore. They dread that 'an anonymous lynch mob' will 'turn up online and make their lives a misery'. He told the BBC: 'I very much fear for the younger generation of writers.'

The suddenness and the effective anonymity of the lynch mob frightens, and the fact that it bays with one voice though many in the mob have not seen the provocation that started it off, only its righteous indignation. These collective actions have consequences, yet there is no way to hold anyone, any group, to account. As a result, the Nobel novelist suggests, writers who are new, or nervous, censor themselves as a precaution. They avoid viewpoints that might raise hackles, they shy away from creating characters outside their immediate experience. He remembered how his first novel 'was written from the point of view of a woman'. *A Pale View of Hills* (1982) is the story of a Japanese mother trying to come to terms with the suicide of her daughter. The book made a mark and Ishiguro was not censured – four decades ago – for appropriation. Would he be let off so lightly today? Is the fact that his new novel features a female robot an attempt to step around a potential mine?

There are such perils! – of being 'boycotted', 'erased', 'cancelled'. It is not only a 'freedom of speech' issue but a challenge to thought and imagination themselves. Negative capability has never been such a treacherous exercise, objective correlatives have never seemed so perilously subjective. Courage is urgently needed and in short supply. Miguel de Unamuno, the Spanish philosopher and rector of the University of Salamanca, is reported to have spoken out at a public meeting. The crowd cheeringly responded to the symbolic cry *Viva la Muerte*. An old man, his copybook not entirely without blot, he rose to his feet: 'Sometimes, to remain silent is to lie, since silence can be interpreted as assent.'

At the level of 'freedom of speech', the amount of traction a relatively small number of social media Savonarola's have achieved is striking. And how cowed those who are themselves deeply invested in the social media have become. One contributor to *PN Review* was subjected to orchestrated social media abuse but, not being a subscriber to Instagram or Facebook, despite the volume and virulence of the action, did not react. The effect was like a military attack waged on a deserted city.

Ishiguro declared, 'If I shrink back from something it's because I would doubt my ability to be able to learn enough about it, to write fairly about it. But, you know, I tend to be quite arrogant about my ability to learn about things, if I put my mind to it.' Such arrogance is earned, not given. 'To learn enough about it, to write fairly about it' is an empowering phrase, a sufficient constraint on the writer who is creating, or essaying, or satirising.

On 9 February, Brian Ferguson reported in the *Scotsman* that Scottish PEN has spoken out against the 'culture of fear' that has developed among Scottish writers as a result of the anti-social perversion of social media, and the 'chilling effect' this has had on Scottish writing. There is 'a need for action to "stem the perpetuation of hatred online" and ensure writers can "express themselves without fear of harassment or violence".'

It is heartening that PEN has taken up the theme unambiguously, speaking of the 'sustained online smearing and harassment' of a Scottish poet. Scotland risked 'the loss of supportive and welcoming communities and the alienation of writers from readers and each other'. There is certainly wariness among writers to engage with supposedly controversial themes for fear of poking an always primed hornets' nest. There is safety from impending collective rage only in right-think and silence. Shaming, cancellation, trolling, exorcism and sanctioned slandering-by-sound-bite are part of the current curtailment of liberty. The techniques are those of extreme orthodoxy disguised as moral alertness and radical correctness. This orthodoxy has somehow rendered itself impregnable to irony.

Ferguson says that Scottish PEN was slow off the mark: a full year passed between the Scottish Poetry Library first raising a particular case and PEN's concerns about 'an escalation, particularly on social media, of disharmony, which is creating fractures that aren't sustainable or healthy in a small country like Scotland'. The delay is part of the 'culture of fear' that has had even institutions dedicated to freedom of expression being worse than cautious in speaking out for individuals who need support. Jenny Lindsay outlined her experience in a memoir, 'Anatomy of a Hounding', published in the *The Dark Horse* in September. Scottish PEN said, 'Jenny's experience speaks to a wider issue in online communities, where a culture of fear leads writers to worry about being abandoned by their peers or implicated by association with others, many second-guessing how their work or even historic online posts could be misconstrued. Writers should feel confident in their ability to express themselves without fear of harassment or violence. We believe harassment in online spaces has a chilling effect on our literary culture.' The question must be, why did it take so long to reach such an obvious conclusion? Where are the other cultural institutions that might be expected to weigh up the evidence and realise that there are many individuals in need of support?

The February issue of *Poetry* magazine, the legendary Chicago institution which was recently editorially transformed by protest into a showcase for diversity, was devoted to publishing work by current and former prisoners. One such prisoner was detained for trafficking in child pornography. He had accumulated so vast a library of obscene material that the police themselves were shocked: 'more than half a million images and films of child sexual abuse,' the *Guardian* reported.

When the magazine was called out, the editors declared, 'it is not our role to further judge or punish [people] as a result of their criminal convictions'. Fair enough: but is it their job to showcase such individuals indiscriminately? The poem was not exceptional; the poet was. Kirk Nesset had been a professor of English literature. He served six years in prison for his offences. The guest editors, said *Poetry*, 'didn't have knowledge of contributors' backgrounds'. '[T]he editorial principle for this issue was to widen access to publication for writers inside prison and to expand access to poetry, bearing in mind biases against and barriers for incarcerated people.' One of the guest editors had herself suffered abuse as a child and was deeply troubled when Professor Nesset's offence was revealed.

The magazine's editors took a high moral tone. They understood the harm sexual offences of this kind did, they said reassuringly, but nonetheless felt justified because the paedophile had served his time. 'As editors, our role is to read poems and facilitate conversations around contemporary poetry.' They want to encourage 'deep and empathetic reading'. Thus the guest editors are exonerated (but also, as it happens, harmed) because they had not been told the contributing poets' crimes; and the editorial hosts are exonerated because they had created a scenario in which anything goes. No room in Chicago for Ishiguro's conscientious pre-requisite, the boringly dutiful necessity 'to learn enough about it, to write fairly about it.'

At the University of Leicester, if you are a medievalist, everything goes. The decision to scrap Beowulf, Chaucer, Gower, Gawain, Langland and much else puts paid to a once distinguished department and to a subject which has, unexpectedly in some cases, enriched readers' – and writers' – lives. A spokeswoman for the University described the new curriculum as 'decolonised' and 'inclusive'.

It was less an ideological than a commercial decision ('a drop in demand from undergraduate and postgraduate students'), approved by engineering specialist Professor Nishan Canagarajah, Chancellor of the University. Medieval literature and English language are dropped because those making decisions are unaware of the depth of English studies, of what constitutes a University discipline. Sixty posts will be cut in 'restructuring' which will offer instead 'excitingly innovative' modules. The spokeswoman insisted that under the current curriculum, 'many reading lists are dominated by white authors. This ignores many great BAME scholars and also means that BAME students do not see themselves reflected in what they are being taught'. But BAME scholars are already doing distinguished innovative work in traditional areas, and BAME writers are already taught on the existing curriculum, and more are added each year.

News and Notes

Queen's Gold Medal 2020

In mid-December The Queen approved the award of Her Majesty's Gold Medal for Poetry to David Constantine. He is the 51st recipient of the award instituted by King George V in 1933 at the suggestion of the then Laureate John Masefield. The Medal Committee commended Constantine this year on the basis of his eleven books of poetry, notably *Collected Poems* (2004), which spans three decades of his work. The Committee is chaired by Poet Laureate Simon Armitage, who himself received the Medal for 2018.

David Constantine made his debut in 1980 with *A Brightness to Cast Shadows*. His publisher, Bloodaxe, was in its second year. Forty years later, they published his eleventh collection. 'Above all,' said Simon Armitage, 'David Constantine is a "humane" poet – a word often used in connection with his work, as if in noticing and detailing the ways of the world he is doing so on behalf of all that is best in us. For over forty years he has shaped a body of work that stands in comparison with that of any of his contemporaries, not just at home but internationally, navigating and negotiating that space between everyday events and their metaphysical or spiritual "otherness".'

Rimbaud's Remains

In recent months controversy has surrounded the final resting place of Arthur Rimbaud's bones. Up until now they have been safely lodged in a family plot in the provincial cemetery at Charleville-Mézières, surrounded by his blood relations. Why are his remains not in the Pantheón, with other great French poets, intellectuals and political leaders? Surely it is because of his irregular, *maudit* relations with Paul Verlaine! President Macron rejected the idea of Rimbaud's remains desecrating the Panteón. The petition launched in September 2020 and signed by thousands of admirers was presidentially rebuffed. The 'lay temple' will not be desecrated. 'I do not wish to contravene the will of the deceased's family,' said the President. (One of Rimbaud's great-great-nieces had opposed the move.) The poet died in 1891, so clearly the family's feelings are a delicate consideration.

The petitioners, including leading politicians and intellectuals, wanted to introduce Rimbaud and Verlaine together in an eternal union, to 'dust down' the temple and to honour 'the bohemian, poetry, and two great homosexuals'. Given the history of their relationship, such a reunion might not have been entirely welcome to them. And some critics of the mischievous petition pointed out that the Pantheón represented all those elements of establishment culture which the truly Bohemian most despises. To introduce the quondam lovers together, others argued, would be 'an Americanisation', a capitulation to 'identity politics' which 'produces hives' in some sectors of French culture. But then the petitioners, seeing Rimbaud surrounded by members of the family from which he fled and which after his death worked to pervert the importance and direction of his *oeuvre*, were moved to righteous pity. 'We must free him from there!' they declared. The petitioners do not intend to give up: 'the hour of a new Pantheón, closer to the French people, more representative of the French people, will inexorably arrive'.

Philippe Jaccottet

Stephen Romer writes: The death of the Swiss poet Philippe Jaccottet at the age of 95 on 25 February marks the end of a generation of poets whose major figures – Yves Bonnefoy, André du Bouchet, Jacques Dupin, and Jaccottet himself – came to maturity in the immediate aftermath of the Second World War. René Char, of an earlier generation, was in many ways their *chef de file*. Char chose to live in relative retirement in Provence, and all four of his *fils spirituels* either did so permanently or had hideaways in rugged areas of the South. It was Char also who in the 1950s and 60s invited Martin Heidegger to Provence to speak on the pre-Socratics , in the famous '*Rencontres sous les marronniers*'. The relation of those philosophers to the elemental was a lasting resource for the French poets, seeking to reconstruct place and meaning. Jaccottet, with these others, and with Paul Celan, was also associated early on with the Galerie Maeght and its house journals. The painterly aesthetics of Miro, Morandi, and most especially of Alberto Giacometti were as crucial to these poets as were, in a different way, the pre-Socratics.

In 1953, Philippe and his young wife the artist Anne-Marie Haesler, moved permanently to the village of Grignan in the Drôme, to the north of Mont Ventoux. Jaccottet was the first of the group to break away from the capital, and he did so, as he explained in interviews, to escape overheated intellectual debate – these were the early years of structuralism, the linguistic turn, *Tel Quel* – that left him feeling more uneasy than ever about his own aims and beliefs. Jaccottet was all his life a seeker and a quester, and the attitude he adopted early on – his second major collection was entitled *L'Ignorant* (1956) – was of modesty and spritual humility: his default position was agnostic, but an agnosticism porous to glimpses of the transcendent, rigorously monitored, and always organically related (as Coleridge might say) to the phenomena of nature.

The classic poem or poetic prose by Jaccottet seems to operate according to a process of tentative forward descriptive movements, almost of *pentimenti*, in which an object perceived, frequently an aspect of the natural world, the kingfisher, the oleander, the robin or, famously, the cherry tree in bloom at the bottom of a ravine, is subjected to a series of comparisons, sometimes in similes of baroque complexity, which disturb the commonly received idea of this poet. These are then summarily discarded, or picked up and applied again, but differently. The approach is apophatic, and proceeds according to a negative theology, a stripping away of everything that can be deemed external to the perceptual task in hand. It is this persistent worrying away at the object, this indefatigable mania for exact description that recalls Francis Ponge, a man whose art would seem on the face of it to be the opposite of Jaccottet's.

What sets Jaccottet apart has to do with tone, the persistent *rappel à l'ordre*, the fear always of getting above himself, of saying too much. Hence, in a brief, beautiful late text, *Couleur de terre* (2009), the aging poet is granted a moment of absolute grace when contemplating a patch of earth, a path leading into the woods – 'a sort of « revelation », if one wishes (if one must) granted, offered to the old and ignorant man that one is'. It is undoubtedly his lyrical attention to landscape – which has its own inquiring rigour – that has made Jaccottet the most widely read and appreciated of these poets in the English-speaking world. He has been well served by poet-translators like Derek Mahon, David Constantine, Mark Treharne, John Taylor, Tess Lewis and Jennie Feldman.

Paradoxes abound when one considers the life and career of Philippe Jaccottet. Born in Moudon in the Suisse Romande he was the most French of Swiss poets. For a writer of 'scrupulous meanness', threatened at every moment by silence and aporia, is collected works form an impressive bulk, as the bible-paper Pléiade edition of 2014 devoted to him attests. Only two other poets have been honoured by a Pléiade in their own lifetimes, Saint-John Perse and René Char. Jaccottet was in fact a tireless man of letters; a copious anthologist, essayist and reviewer, his writings on art are only now about to appear from Le Bruit du Temps, the publishing house run by his son, Antoine. He was also a prodigious translator, of Hölderlin, Rilke, Musil, but also of Homer, Mandelstam, Gongora and Leopardi.

Barbara Köhler

Evelyn Schlag writes: Barbara Köhler had green fingers as a gardener and, by extension, as a poet. She dug in the recesses of the German language, harked back to their etymologies and uncovered hidden meanings. She was also a kind of (and kind) betrayer, telling her readers about the mysteries of word families. By adding a pronoun or changing a case she created new idioms, as in her most famous poem about German unification, *Rondeau Allemagne* of 1994: 'Ich harre aus im Land und geh *ihm* fremd.' That 'ihm', a *dativus ethicus*, includes the emotion of a strong belonging as well as disillusion. Hers was a very intimate relationship with language. Her volume *Blue Box* has this epigraph: 'I am talking to language. Sometimes it answers. Other times somebody else does.'

It comes as no surprise that she would translate Gertrude Stein. *Tender Buttons* are resurrected as 'Zarte knöpft', not simply Zarte Knöpfe. She takes the liberty of converting German grammatical categories by supplying the cores of words with prefixes and suffixes they have never had. In her own texts (which she considered untranslatable) she used English words because they yielded new associations, thus 'movie' in a German text simultaneously means film, cinema and movement. 'Newspaper' is a nice contrast to the German Altpapier, (waste paper, scrap paper), which in effect are mostly stacks of old newspapers.

In *Niemands Frau* (*Nobody's Wife*), her take on the Odyssey, she tells the story from a female perspective and foregrounds the women's experiences. Her distrust of philosophers such as Lacan is visceral, she once confessed to getting a belly-ache from his sentences but admitted it might be a problem of translation. She had an unerring sensibility for the mechanisms of political speech when language is abused as an instrument of power. Political speech always wants to suggest consent, claim majority, isolate dissent.

Barbara Köhler was born in Burgstädt, East Germany, in 1959. She worked in textile production and in an old people's home before studying at the Johannes R. Becher Institute of Literature in Karl-Marx-Stadt/Chemnitz. Her first collection of poetry, *Deutsches Roulette*, was published in 1991. From 1994 onwards she lived in Duisburg, collaborating with visual artists in text-space installations, teaching as Writer-in-Residence at, among other places, Warwick. She was awarded the prestigious Clemens von Brentano Prize and the Peter Huchel Prize. On January 8th she died at the age of 61.

Mahmud Kianush

Giles Goodland writes: I first encountered Mahmud Kianush though his books. I had moved to a leafy corner of West London, and browsing in the local library, found an unusually full representation of his work, all published by Rockingham Press. Intrigued, I emailed the publisher. A day later I was sitting with Mahmud drinking strong coffee in what would become our regular meeting place on Pitshanger Lane. He turned out to be the best possible conversationalist, lively, quick-thinking, obsessed with poetry's relation to the Big Themes. He had rejected the Islamic teachings he had been brought up with. Such was his dislike of theocracy, he did not let me use the word 'Iranian'. But he never rejected the rich tradition of Persian poetry.

Born in 1934 in Mashhad, he soon moved to Tehran. He became a well-known poet of a modernist slant, and became estranged from the expectation that he write poetry pleasing to the masses or the state. Perhaps sensing the coming crisis in his country, he took early retirement from the civil service and settled in London with his wife Pari Mansour, also a writer and translator, and their two children, in 1976. There he formed a close connection with the BBC's Persian section, and wrote and edited prodigiously, translating Steinbeck, Lawrence, Césaire, Beckett, Fugard, Lagerkvist, Lorca, Cavafy and others into Persian, and many Persian poets into English, editing anthologies, and writing his own poetry both in English and Persian.

As the years passed, he became frailer. Still immaculately dressed, he started using a Zimmer frame. At the beginning of 2020, he was diagnosed with leukaemia. In spring, his wife Pari died of Covid. From that time, he was only animated by the idea of putting together his final book, but was discouraged by the news that his Rockingham editor had ceased publishing. We could not meet for coffee, but by phone and email we assembled his last book, *The Journey*, now published by Knives Forks and Spoons Press. A rigorous editor to the end, the book went through several changes. In our last conversation he was still worried about a single missing line-space. While in hospital for his cancer, he contracted Coronavirus, and died on the 12th of January.

He will be missed very much by his two children, Kaveh and Katy, and by myself, his son in poetry, as he described me, and by Joanne Arnott, his daughter in poetry.

Colin Falck

Paul McLoughlin writes: After gaining first degrees in PPE and in philosophy, psychology and physiology at Magdalen College, Oxford in the 1950s, Colin Falck (1934–2020) helped Ian Hamilton and others to found the influential poetry magazine *the Review* in 1962, acting as deputy editor for its duration, and going on to be poetry editor of *The New Review.* It might be said that while not seeking the limelight, Falck provided the philosophical framework that enabled Hamilton to espouse and support a new kind of imagism, one that paid the closest attention to allowing poems to reveal the nature of reality. I learned from Martin Dodsworth that Frank Kermode was highly impressed by a 1968 Falck essay in *the Review*, 'Poetry and Wittgenstein'. In 1988, he was awarded a PhD in Literary Theory at the University of London. He worked in various British and American universities. Most of the latter were in the universities' London Programmes, but also included York College of Pennsylvania.

Falck contributed poems and reviews to early issues of *PN Review* (including three poems and a review of Peter Jones's 'Imagist Poetry' to *Poetry Nation One* in 1973) and went on later to provide articles on Robinson Jeffers (1987) and Edna St Vincent Millay (1992), two 'unfashionable' poets, editing *Selected Poems* for both for Carcanet.

In *Myth, Truth and Literature: Towards a True Post-Modernism* (1989; 1994) Falck mounted a sustained assault on the language theories of Saussure, Derrida et al. Taking his cue from German Romantic Philosophy and, particularly, Shelley's *Defence of Poetry*, he railed against insistences that found no room for the meaning-creation, the 'probing-into-obscurity', that he took to be the defining characteristic and *raison d'etre* of language. In the hands of Saussure, he believed, language became, in Shelley's words, 'dead to all the nobler purposes of human intercourse' and facilitated 'the now almost universal tendency to value literary criticism or literary theory on a level with, or even above' literary art itself. It also led to the immersive academization of poetry. Camille Puglia hailed the book as one that 'reveals the future of literary criticism'. In *American and British Verse in the Twentieth Century: The Poetry that Matters* (2003), Falck asks 'Why is it that almost no one can quote more than a few words from any American or British poet since (say) Robert Lowell or Philip Larkin?' Edna St Vincent Millay was not taught at universities because her work was deemed to contain nothing that needed deciphering or unfolding in seminar groups and was therefore regarded as too simple to bother with. And Robinson Jeffers was similarly rejected because the poet's views on man and the natural world were deemed unpalatable, but both remained very fine poets. What was needed if poetry were to save itself from its 'current' self was a 'Middlebrow Revival'. This was not an argument against complexity, rather it was opposed to self-regarding verse that took readers into the poet's mind and made no attempt to show what it felt like to be alive in the world. Poetry, in short, needed 'to re-connect with the lives of ordinary educated people', and poets to learn again how to make their lines 'sing'.

Falck's own poetry was published in two early pamphlets (under the imprint of *the Review*); a first full collection with Carcanet, *Backwards into the Smoke* (1973), two further collections for Stride (1992 and 1997) and finally a near-posthumous volume from Shoestring Press just before he died. He was instrumental in helping other poets on their way, through the Hampstead Poetry Workshops that began in Thurlow Road in 1985 and continued until he was unable through illness to attend. Declan Ryan's fine poem, 'i.m. Colin Falck', reveals much about the flavour of the group's meetings. Over the years its members included the likes of Hugo Williams, Jo Shapcott, Ruth Padel, and Michael Donaghy: the list stretches on with any number of other poets who deserve mention. It is difficult to recall any who were less than accomplished. The range and approaches of its poets are a testament to Falck's inclusiveness. An old battered foolscap manila envelope was where all attending placed copies of their own anonymous poem. Each person in turn would take one such poem out of the envelope, distribute it, read it aloud, and it would be discussed. This 'anonymity', such as it was, meant even the brightest of stars had to endure an occasional mauling. Each discussion ended, as Ryan's poem does, with Falck asking, 'Any more angles on this one?' At which point the poet would reveal their identity. The envelope (the original from 1985), surely deserves to be preserved in an archive somewhere. It is a significant artefact in the recent history of British and Irish poetry.

Joan Margarit

Bloodaxe Books announced: The Catalan poet Joan Margarit (1938–2021), who had been suffering from cancer, died in February.

One of Spain's major modern writers, he was born in 1938 in Sanaüja, La Segarra region, in Catalonia. An architect as well as a poet, from 1968 until his retirement he was Professor of Structural Calculations at Barcelona's Technical School of Architecture, working for part of that time on Gaudí's Sagrada Família cathedral.

He first published poetry in Spanish, but after four books decided to write in Catalan. From 1980 he began to build his reputation as a major Catalan poet. As well as publishing many collections in Catalan, he published Spanish versions of all his work, and over the past twenty years gained recognition as a leading poet in Spanish. The melancholy and candour of his poetry remind readers of Thomas Hardy, whose work he translated.

He received many of the main awards available to Spanish writers, including in 2019 the Reina Sofía Prize for Ibero-American Poetry, the most important poetry award for Spain, Portugal and Latin America, and in the same year the Cervantes Prize.

Jean Valentine

The American poet Jean Valentine, winner of the National Book Award and a Pulitzer Prize finalist, died on 29 December. She was 86. Her characteristic poetic structure – taut, clear free verse images culminating in an emotional thrust – a minimalism reduced to cliché by some of the popular Instagram poets who have followed in her wake – earned her many readers in her six-decade career, and over an impressive library of fourteen collections. Seamus Heaney evoked her manner: 'rapturous, risky, shy of words but desperately true to them'. Each stanza of the poem builds to a climax, and the final poem is a succession of precisions, cumulative and stripped of context. 'Mother and Child, Body and Soul' (the two pairings juxtaposed, without conjunctions) begins: '*Child*/ You've boarded me over like a window or a well.' This startling image is returned to after a life story rendered in three brief stanzas: 'And this child, this/ window in my side,/ boarded over all my life,/—how can I take the boards off, in this wind?/ I will break if I bend...' Window, or well? Mother, or body? Child, or soul? The *New York Times* obituary spoke of her economy, images 'so concise they could seem like fragments. It was the immediacy of emotion she was after, and she often found it in dreamscapes.' Alice Quinn, who loved her poems and often printed them in the *New Yorker*, said, 'She was brilliant at evoking the power of love and the endlessness, the indwelling aspect of eternity that we feel.'

Lawrence Ferlinghetti

Peter Pegnall writes: There was both more and less to this centenarian poet than meets the eye. He was a tall, imposing figure, whose impeccable manners lent greater force to his presence. At the same time, he relished farce and absurdity, in his later years resembling part of a comedy routine with his dear fellow communist, Jack Hirschman, diminutive, sporting an heroic moustache and a Stetson. Lasting so long is a measure of the man's good judgment, his canny business sense, his courage and lack of apocalyptic delusions.

As a bookseller, he navigated The City Lights Bookshop through years of turbulence, social and financial. He had met George Whitman in Paris in the late 1940s and witnessed the establishment near Le Pont Neuf of *Le Mistral,* far more than just a bookshop, a café, a temporary lodging house for scribblers, a beating heart of Bohemia and simply a quiet place to read and talk. Ferlinghetti followed this example and opened 'The City Lights', a tribute to Chaplin and a reflection of its owner's battle against the authoritarian and the pompous. It is amazing that both Shakespeare and Company (the inherited name of *Le Mistral*) and *City Lights* survived and thrive. It goes without saying that independent bookshops can be the life blood of writers, those solitary sociable animals, often hopeless with money and marriage. Ferlinghetti was not unaware of his need for an anchor: in 1971, the distinguished librarian Nancy Peters assumed administrative and financial responsibility. A risk taker, Ferlinghetti was also a realist.

As a publisher, he devised the *Pocket Poets*, four by six inches, just the right size and price for the lonesome hobo, the penniless dissident. The list of poets is astonishing: Carlos Williams, Lowry, Burroughs, O'Hara, Rexroth, Levertov, Prévert, Patchen, Duncan and, most significantly for the future of the publishing house, Ginsberg. It was the botched prosecution of Ginsberg's *Howl* in 1957 that gave the book and its publishers the most effective publicity they could have wished. *Howl* remains the most successful of City Lights' texts, with more than fifty reprints. Ferlinghetti's sense of history was confirmed by his letter offering Ginsberg publication: 'I greet you at the beginning of a great career', consciously echoing Emerson's endorsement of Walt Whitman. He went on to ask, 'when can I expect the manuscript?'

Despite being seen as a godfather of 'The Beats' Ferlinghetti denied membership. Many movements achieve identity retrospectively, but there is a special validity to Ferlinghetti's insistence. To begin with, he was a successful scholar, a fluent linguist, a skipper on a submarine chaser during D-Day action and a lifelong pacifist as a result of witnessing the aftermath of the bomb at Nagasaki. All this from a boy born in Yonkers whose father may have died before his birth and whose mother spent most of her life in an asylum. A tough as well as a sensitive man, then, who was never especially taken with narcotics or dope. He dropped a few tabs but was by no devotee of astral adventures or self-destruction. His long life was not a matter of chance.

His poetry and his political convictions were also very much his own. His sense of irony was acute, without vitiating sincerity or force. His *Autobiography* is an often hilarious 'Essay on an American', full of literary allusions and topographical detail. He really doesn't let himself off the hook:

(I have) seen the Cities of the Plain
And wallowed in the wilds of West-
  chester
With its roving bands of natives
In stationwagons.
I have seen them.
I am the man.
I was there.
I suffered
somewhat.

'The Cities of the Plain' in Genesis are Sodom and Gomorrah and Westchester is a picture book rural suburb of New York. The Clintons live there now; so did Billy Collins, so wild west it is. And how this poet raises an eyebrow.

A lifetime campaigner against the motor car and all its depredations, his assaults can be brilliantly mordant:

on the nickelodeon a cowboy ballad
  groans
'got myself a Cadillac' the cowhand
  moans.
He didn't get it in Cuba, baby'
(one thousand fearful words for Fidel
  Castro)

The poems defy categorisation: often rhetorical, but also tender, lyrical, visual, wry, surprising. There is much to be said for that Lawrence Ferlinghetti. I'd like to suggest that he is a still kicking refutation of Robert Frost's self-satisfied little squib: 'I never dared be radical when young / For fear it would make me conservative when old.'

Ferlinghetti dared. Rock on, Larry.

Reports

Fire and Tears: A Meditation

VAHNI CAPILDEO

The world is on fire. News of fires comes flying from poet and non-poet friends alike: not fires of scandal, but a tornado of fire in the US, the estimated death or displacement of perhaps three billion animals in Australia's bush fires, and a landmark tree standing on Lady Chancellor Hill in Trinidad where my friend and I used to walk, still the shape of itself, but largely charcoal. John Kinsella, at an online event at the University of Warwick (November 2020), spoke of his hands-on work creating and maintaining firebreaks, and planting trees. Introducing the poetry readings and symposium for *Plumwood Mountain* journal's 'Writing in the Pause' issue, Jonathan Skinner noted it could be called 'Writing in the Fire'. Skinner's introduction takes up this theme, pointing to the sameness as well as difference of the fires of ecological and sociopolitical violence. He quotes James Baldwin: 'Do I really want to be integrated into a burning house?'

According to people with a good internet connection, amiable faces, and eyesight that tolerates Zoom, we are integrated, or bricked up into, our houses as never before, while the pandemic flares around us. The office-house is a place of relative safety and comfort. It burns only as a hearth, a comfortable gathering-place... unless fire is hurled at it, unfairly. I shall return to this notion, which is acquiring the status of truth by virtue of repetition. First, a little more on fire.

Fire was integrated into my childhood house in the Americas as the Hindu god, Agni. When blue gas flared under the iron griddle, sometimes my mother or father would speak a Sanskrit formula, or at least Agni's name. A miniature roti, if roti was on the menu (it wasn't every day), was offered to him. Years later I saw a woman priest similarly invoke the Orisha god Shango when lighting incense. Fire was a sharp friend you learnt to handle. As I was small enough, sometimes I was tasked with crawling into the oven and lighting the gas. My earliest memories involve soaking earthenware lamps in water, preparing cotton wicks, and lighting rows of them, one from another, flame to flame, sometimes 300, for the Hindu New Year. When my father was cremated in an open-air pyre, a piece of white camphor was placed under his tongue. My brother lit it with a long bamboo torch: the final filial act of care. This disposal may seem cruel, but in Hinduism the body after death is like a soiled garment no longer needed. One of the presiding priests cited other Sanskrit names for fire, differentiating between the purifier and the destroyer.

I see fire, even destruction by fire, through the eyes of a child of a culture of fire. Burning can be integrated into the house, part of our domestic and spiritual ecology. The supreme yogi, Lord Shiva, famously turned distractions to ash with the concentrated heat of his third eye.

One week this winter, a close-reading group in Edinburgh looked at the Gospel of Matthew and the parable of the ten wise and foolish bridesmaids, or virgins. All ten took lamps, but only five took oil. They all fell asleep, and the bridegroom arrived at midnight. The foolish ones failed to borrow oil from the wise ones; they had to go shopping, making them late for the feast. When they arrived, the bridegroom would not let them in. He told them solemnly, 'I do not know you'. There was much discussion of how being off guard is not the same as being wilfully underprepared; of the rights and wrongs of sharing in different situations, and what things we cannot share, but must seek and do for ourselves.

Naturally, it was the fire that caught my imagination. It reminded me of helping with preparations for a Vedic Hindu wedding. We needed many days, and were wildly excited when the groom's party arrived, as is traditional, at the bride's house for the final ceremony, which includes the couple walking around a fire, tied to each other by the wrist, facing the sun and becoming inhabited by the divine masculine and feminine. How far was the New Testament groom's party travelling, perhaps in the dark or through wilderness? Without enough lamplight, perhaps they would lose their way. Even if they were bringing their own lamps, would they feel welcomed if they were not met with lamps? How else would illumination be mutual? For when you hurry out carrying a lamp, looking for the bright face of the bridegroom, your own face and path will be lit up. Perhaps having enough oil means having lived in a way that recognisably places you on the side of love. Perhaps it means making sure others don't get lost while you and your friends are disputing resources.

When I think of fire, I also think of tears. Sitting masked and distanced on a Cambridge riverbank, two non-white women friends and I asked the usual catch-up questions. How is your family? Have you seen any nice cats? Has anyone cried at you lately? If you do not know what I mean, perhaps you have been insufficiently cried at. Here are two examples of weaponised tears, one from literature and one from life. In *Henry VIII* Act II Scene IV, Katherine of Aragon is on trial. She warns Wolsey: 'My drops of tears / I'll turn to sparks of fire'. He counsels patience. She calls this out as tone-policing. 'You are mine enemy', she declares, denying that he can be her judge. However, Katherine's sense of her rights derives from her sense that she is royalty, not that people seeking justice commonly deserve to speak and be heard. The second example occurred at dinner after an event where I was an invited speaker. The organiser, a friend, caught my eye. She passed on a question from a translator guest: *where had I learnt English? I spoke it very well.* I looked at the questioner and gently challenged the grounds of the question. She stood up at table, like a golden lily, weeping with indignation while saying she was perfectly right to ask. She kept standing, insisting, and weeping. Her words hurt me. Her performance as vulnerable flesh made me wrong in my very body, like stone, for keeping my cool and wanting my dinner. Those crystalline tears blistered me. Being in company who could laugh at those tears would have performed a third-eye function: evaporating them. Otherwise, the tears stick and burn like pitch.

The phrase 'white-women tears' sounds tasteless and divisive. Yet how many readers share this experience of not infrequently being cried at? What interests me is the rupture in a dialogue that changes, in a professional or public context, from an equal exchange of words to the forced, shared witness of personal discomfort elevated to spectacular pain; and which bodies are turned by grief into a thing for a pedestal, not a thing to be tidied away. Paradoxically, in these cases, the apparently suffering body is the one that spoke hurtful words. The person at whom hurtful words were launched now is required, for the sake of amiability, to find comforting words to staunch the tears that have been launched. Crying is a form of setting what makes you uncomfortable on fire. It obliterates. It shows an individual sense of entitlement, a willingness to burn the house of conversation down.

My good internet connection found me and my faulty eyesight at a Zoom meeting listening to a speaker on the gaze. According to her, we are accustomed to looking out and to looking at. Now our houses are our shadow-play caves as we try to be present via the internet; and being masked if we do meet is a new deprivation. Almost everyone who had chosen to share their video showed rapt and amiable faces. This was in the eleventh month of the pandemic; for me, the eighth month of hearing paid professionals discourse on the office-house as a retreat, and enclosure as a rupture with the normal. Yet I was conscious that at least one listener not sharing their video was housebound by disability, not lockdown.

Suddenly I had a swooping vision of many years' and two hemispheres' worth of incarcerated people: migrants trapped on small islands in Scandinavia, the Mediterranean, the Pacific; detention centres in the neighbourhood of business-and-holiday British airports; crippled poor relations languishing in small rooms in the Caribbean and Latin America, where the state assumes 'the family' looks after its own. I 'saw' East Asian urbanites donning medical masks against pollution and winter flu. Sweaty bandanas were pulled up over dusty, filmic American desert faces. In memory, the roadside tea vendor in old Calcutta who communicated by flashing his eyes over the geometric scarf sheltering nose and mouth from the cold wind flashed his eyes at me again, urging me to speak.

My heart forcefully told me: visibility is a privilege. The expectation of being seen and known has hardened into scales that do not fall from 'our' eyes. Why not catch fire? Why not rush to find 'our' identity with the hidden ones instead... with the long-time masked? I put an ultra-condensed version of this in the Zoom chat box. The answer? What I had said was 'brilliant ... we in the west need to learn ... We in the west have a lot to learn'. How did 'west' vs 'east' even enter the discussion? Katherine of Aragon's tears transmute into flame so far as her queenly quality is perceived. My foreign quality whited out the re-visioning I proposed. The adjective 'brilliant', detached from any engagement, translates as 'extra; optional, esoteric, distant and sometime-perhaps-never-to-come'. To be seen was to be mis-known, placed as oppositional, as being of the 'east'. I stayed quiet. From experience of similar situations, I was afraid one of the good faces would cry or otherwise perform discomfort as pain. Tears are not mine to shed; my spirit returned a NO OIL TO SPARE error.

Will Harris, in *Rendang* (Granta, 2020), shows himself to be a poet of love and vision, who knows the world is on fire. His astonishing poem 'Break' opens with the speaker's attempt to revive a dead tree by feeding it with coffee grounds. This gesture of emptying out as part of a cycle of nourishment, a work of faith more than hope, leads into a reflection on what it might mean to be 'fine' while being 'on a break' from one's beloved. The stanza seems to carry out the digestion, or diffusion, of the steam and bitterness of yesterday's coffee, along with unreported conversations. Primarily it records an openness to processes of transformation. The second stanza cites the Book of Job, Sharon Olds, and jazz 'breaks'. This compound music of breakage accompanies the speaker saying 'I'm aware of / something in me broken. That doesn't mean unhappy'. The third and final stanza explores the break as in-betweenness:

> You slip into the break and look around, see past
> and future,
> love and sickness rearranged. *Reordered*. You feel
> yourself
> both whole and breached. As me you. As you do.

Pronouns disturb each other's territory in this syntax, so that being and doing, self and other, are in an unwonted state of intimacy and change. The poem concludes with trans-human tenderness, wondering about the consciousness of dying dogs, and whether it's 'like daylight breaking through an open door'. Not seeking likeness, Harris neither enforces nor condemns integration. By embracing absence, he embraces presence and loss. Without figuring internal adjustment as imposed, or external change as disastrous, his tearless yet vulnerable poetics of patience moves from heat to light, coming around to dawn.

Analog Sea and the Pixelated Madness

Horatio Morpurgo

'Technology is the knack of so arranging the world that we don't have to experience it', wrote Max Frisch in 1957. In an essay published only after his death in 2015, Oliver Sacks reflected on the ubiquitous use of smartphones in his New York neighbourhood. He foresaw 'a neurological catastrophe' as the reflexes of a generation with 'no immunity to the seductions of digital life' are conditioned in this way. Two Norwegian reports, recently cited by Will Self, studied the effect of social media use on the ability to 'lose oneself' in long-form prose narrative. They suggested that *Homo virtualis* is already with us: 'I can see', wrote Self, 'no future for words printed on paper... if our civilisation continues on this digital trajectory'.

The *Analog Sea Review*, founded in 2018 by the poet Jonathan Simons, is part of an 'offline publishing house and institute'. It offers 'life-sustaining counter-measures to the pixelated madness'. The above quotations all come from work that has appeared in its pages. It is published in English but in Freiburg. The Central European atmosphere of its content extends also to its elegant hardback design. 'When you express yourself, use the things around you', wrote Rilke, in his *Letters to a Young Poet*. 'If your everyday life seems poor, do not blame it; blame yourself; tell yourself that you are not poet enough to call forth its riches.'

Analog Sea faces the worst about the likely prospect of 'downgraded humans misusing upgraded computers to wreak havoc on themselves and the world'. It turns to poets and artists, living and dead, to novelists, physicists, psychoanalysts, film-makers and philosophers, not only for their views on the pixelated madness, but for hints on how our relationship to primary experience could be restored.

Novelty of course has always been the internet's chief promise and selling point. Are we too quick to take that novelty on trust? There are longer stories to tell in which the internet is neither as new nor as exciting as its marketing people would relentlessly have us believe. It represents an acceleration of that tendency described by Guy Debord, half a century ago, which he called 'the spectacle'. Part of *Analog Sea*'s 2019 edition was devoted to Debord's current relevance.

The spectacle is the reign of personalities, 'news', commodified art, a reign of appearances under which no 'central question' can any longer be posed. It is the power of all this to hold us spellbound. It controls our lives by reconstituting us as passive spectators, so long as we remain ignorant of it. Dextrously, it determines how we relate both to the life going on around us and within us. It is the 'ruling order's defence': it serves capitalist structures by acting as the veil which conceals them even as it distracts us.

If 'the entertaining celebrity is a capitalist robot', as the philosopher Donald Kuspit has more recently argued, then what is the country which elects such a robot to highest office? Debord's answer was neither scream nor shrug. It was the '*dérive*': literally, 'drifting', a reinvention of the way we engage with our surroundings so as to subvert this omnipresent 'ideology of trade'.

In developing his idea, Debord drew on the Surrealists, the Romantics and the Baroque, as well as from the Age of Chivalry and its traditions of the long journey of adventure and discovery. He affirmed, in other words, a rich vocabulary of pre-spectacular dissent on which we might still be drawing. There's a reason we are encouraged at every turn to play down the past while we cry up the Novelty.

'Industrial societies turn their citizens into image junkies', Susan Sontag wrote in *On Photography* (1977), 'it is the most irresistible form of mental pollution.' The impact of television's commercial images was an early theme in Wim Wenders's work. The director is interviewed in the third (2020) issue about how digital technology has taken over where television left off and where that leaves a film-maker who wants to stay thoughtful.

'Anybody who says digital technology makes everything easier doesn't know what they're talking about', he complains. 'It's easier to shoot, but you end up with ten times more material.' Some film scores 'already sound as if an algorithm has written them'. Readers of *Emotion Pictures* will already be aware that Wenders is a writer. He speaks here about how much reading has mattered.

The issues are made up of several sections, artwork announcing each new theme. After Wenders, for example, comes Glenn Gould. The reclusive pianist made a series of 'contrapuntal documentaries', experimental films, about the Arctic as an 'archetype for human solitude'. A transcript of one of them is followed by an aphorism from Pascal. Reflections from environmental writers on the Arctic lead up to Gould's commencement speech to a group of Canadian students in 1964.

Analog Sea's editors insist they are not 'anti-technological'. They use the internet 'almost daily'. Their dispute is with technology's 'promises of endless amusement and togetherness' and how in practice this 'digital utopianism continues to pull us deeper into dark waters'. You can, to put it another way, hate car culture and still drive one of the damn things.

The review asks what a 'society devoid of interiority' would be like, if that is indeed where this digital dance is leading. About its implications for self-knowledge, it asks Michel de Montaigne. 'The call to solitude is universal', wrote Thomas Merton. But where do we find it now? For the meaning of leisure in such a world, it turns to Freiburg-trained philosopher Byung-Chul Han (a discovery I was glad of). Walter Benjamin once called boredom 'the dream bird that hatches the egg of experience.'. Can that bird survive Instagram?

Analog Sea feels here and there like last-ditch fighting, but maybe that's how the worthwhile battles always feel. American and British poets are preponderant but that's just a quibble. In the midst of home-schooling, Brexit and Donald Trump's attempted putsch, I was profoundly grateful for this view out of a window in Freiburg.

Zoom's the Ticket

CAROLINE CLARK

The excitement or willingness with which you might sign up for a Zoom reading surely depends on your personal circumstances. For me, it's such a rare thing to be able to attend a reading, I'm with the more willing. As I wait to be let into the 'meeting' it all comes back to me: the joy of culture in the present moment. No fast-forwarding, no pause button.

Once in, depending on the set-up, you may see the other attendees' screens flicking on – either as a black space, if they don't have their video on, or with their faces and backgrounds visible. Carcanet's readings don't reveal the other attendees or show their screens, but we are told there's time at the start to use the 'chat' function to 'say hello'. I stay silent but am interested to see so-and-so's there. What does it mean to reveal myself here and say hello? I'm overthinking this. I have not developed Zoom social skills yet. I am a hermit in from the cold. I will need to learn how to behave myself. Wow – there are people here from all over the world. Wow – I am seeing faces/names of people who have only ever existed in contents pages. I really should stay silent. In fact, we all stay silent. Good Zoom housekeeping rule no. 1: mute the attendees (or get them to mute themselves, depending on format). Are we viewers, participants or the audience? One reader at a Russian poetry event attempts to formalise the relationship, telling us: you are the voyeur. But theory thuds against the window as we stand to switch the kettle on.

Zoom readings are flourishing now through necessity; viewer etiquette is developing very fast. Over the past year, Carcanet's Zoom readings have gradually established a most effective format. Front of house is the welcoming Jazmine Linklater, who explains how Zoom works to newcomers: how to use the chat and Q&A functions, and gives an idea of the reading and interview time. She then hands over to the host (such as the excellent John Clegg) who introduces the poet. We see the host again after the reading to interview the poet and pose selected audience questions. The natural intimacy of a Zoom reading means it's easy to quickly make friends with the viewers, who are in turn encouraged to join in by sending comments through the chat function (though I wish at times I could stop them popping up during the reading).

It is remarkable that Zoom does not kill the magic of conversation or the sense of community among those interested in the same thing. A bit of spontaneous, real-time banter between the host and poet is a treat – especially in these times. Some readers are of course better at reading their own work than others; some have personalities that come across very well in this potentially intimate format. I like the provision of the page via a screen share where possible. Regarding this, Michael Schmidt comments: '[it's] something on which I insisted because we are book publishers and we are presenting text backed by voice and trying not to foreground "personality"'. It helps the viewer to focus on the poems and gives an immediate sense of what kind of poems these are (so useful, for example, at the launch of Evan Jones's absorbing *Later Emperors*). For those who don't want to see the page, they can simply click to make the reader's face bigger.

The smaller presses tend to have less structured events and use the format which allows for the attendees' screens to be visible. Attendees can then choose whether to keep their videos on or off; if off, their names will still be visible. This makes for an even greater sense of community and it's fun to flick through the faces/names. Sometimes the session is left open after a reading and attendees can hang around to chat.

Whatever the format, a good introduction to the poet and book is essential. Some readings that cut to the poet too quickly can leave the uninitiated viewer feeling distanced. Aidan Semmens, creator of the online magazine *Molly Bloom* and a series of associated readings, sets a wonderfully informal yet focused tone in his introductions, and – like John Clegg – he exudes real enthusiasm for the books and poets in question. Highlights from *Molly Bloom* readings (see the YouTube channel '*Molly Bloom* poetry') include Dorothy Lehane and Elinor Cleghorn's captivating, screen-flicking collaboration *With Sequelae*, Geraldine Monk's slot, Alan Baker's Tyneside dialect poems and Maria Stadnicka's reading.

I had heard that I should try to catch a reading by Petero Kalulé and, thanks to Guillemot Press/Chener Books, I was glad to have been able to watch Petero read with flute, piano and bells. Luke Thompson of Guillemot has felt online readings long coming: 'I think a lot of venues and events haven't had the confidence or time in the past to face up to the potential of these technologies ... Now we're all having to get to grips with the technology and hopefully this will mean when we go back to live events again organisers will feel more confident incorporating Zoom or Teams or whatever.' Guillemot Press have a reading a month planned so far up to June 2021.

Zoom launch readings certainly don't need to have smooth edges. They are a sharing, rather than a performance. Carcanet charges £2 to attend a live launch, which is then reimbursed on purchase of the book – or you can watch the reading for free when it's put on their YouTube channel. *Tears in the Fence* was quick to organise its 2020 festival on Zoom. They had a suggested donation per session or one for the whole programme. Recordings from the festival are being released gradually on their website and YouTube channel.

Over these past months of online poetry viewing, I feel my sense of the poetry coming out of these isles has grown. But has it really? My sense of what's on offer virtually has certainly grown. Some presses have been quicker to bite the Zoom bullet than others. With a small press doing a launch to an audience of over fifty a few days ago, it certainly seems worth it. The greatest benefit of this format is of course accessibility. I have travelled much further, virtually – and heard a greater range of vowels – across England than train ticket prices would normally allow. And borders have been painlessly crossed: to Italy, North America, Russia and Israel.

At the moment we are on new ground and a willingness remains to be cultivated among certain viewers. As word spreads, my guess is that even those who never thought they'd attend an online reading will try. I've usually been notified of upcoming Zoom readings through Facebook. But knowing about a reading doesn't guarantee attendance. Ultimately, the only real engagement-advancing algorithm is interest or at least open-mindedness. It takes just one enjoyable reading with a beverage of choice to adopt a new habit. While many feel there is no substitute for in-person readings with a live atmosphere, certainly, in terms of accessibility, Zoom wins. I do wonder though whether attendance at a Zoom reading will gradually substitute, rather than encourage, a deeper engagement with the book. As with everything, time (and the publishers) will tell.

January 2021

On Bringing Out Hamish Whyte's Memoir of Edwin Morgan

HELENA NELSON

When Hamish Whyte asked whether I'd be interested in publishing a memoir about his thirty-year friendship with Edwin Morgan, of course I said yes. My enthusiasm was offset by one concern. Should a key contribution to Morgan lore be brought out by such a small press as Happen*Stance*? For me, Morgan is one of the giants.

But there's a sense in which I *was* the right publisher for *Morgan & Me*. An enduring relationship sits at the core of this book, and many professional endeavours rely on such connections. When I started publishing in 2005, Hamish Whyte (Mariscat Press owner/editor), was particularly generous with his time, wisdom and practical suggestions. I learned much from him. He told me stories about poets he had worked with, stories that aren't publicly told. I came to know his own poems too, and relished their precision, lucidity and playfulness. It was a privilege to publish *Hannah, Are You Listening?* in 2013, and *Now the Robin* five years later. Hamish is a naturally reticent person. I knew he wouldn't take on a prose memoir easily or lightly.

So I was encouraging about the memoir, which complements Jim McGonigal's 2012 biography, *Beyond The Last Dragon: A Life of Edwin Morgan*. But Whyte's account adds affecting human detail. It's an openly personal story, revealing much about both writer and subject. For me, it was richly educative. It took me back to Morgan's work (the Carcanet *Centenary Selected* being a marvellous source) and to Whyte's own development as a poet and publisher in the Glasgow poetry scene of the 70s and 80s. It captures evanescent detail through postcards, photographs, jokes, shared lunches, joys and sorrows. The older poet, with no children of his own, gradually becomes an honorary member of the Whyte family. After he and Hamish's wife, Winifred, are diagnosed with cancer 'almost simultaneously' in 1999, they compare treatments. At Winifred's funeral, 'Eddie was late arriving, because his taxi driver couldn't find the place, and he sat at the back. I turned round at one point and saw he was crying'.

Morgan & Me is moving in the best sense, an affecting tribute from a unique perspective. It covers the sort of range that only a poet-publisher could write about – from the nitty-gritty of the editing process to the 'absinthe-with-Eddie' sessions (a joy for Eddie; a mixed blessing for Hamish). We read about Morgan's attitudes to love and loss, his optimism and his regret, his coming out as a gay man, his incorrigible delight in falling in love again in his seventies. All of this gives a special context to certain poems, something to treasure.

For example, in the *Centenary Selected*, there's a poem inauspiciously titled: 'To the Librarians, H. W. and H. H.'. It reflects the experience of donating literary papers to the Glasgow Mitchell Library for what would become the Edwin George Morgan archive. What an apparently dry topic! The initials belong to Hamish Whyte and Henry Heaney, and the experience of gathering these papers and gradually compiling a Morgan bibliography is described in the memoir. For Whyte, who had been 'infected by the bibliography bug', it was a 'Holy Grail' opportunity to get to know one of his heroes. For Morgan, the sharing of private documents was 'peeling layer on layer like a flaying'. It brought the two men close, not least because such detail was personal – and that which is personal is always risky.

And so was writing *Morgan & Me* for Hamish Whyte. In his prologue to the memoir, he notes that such writing is 'as much about its writer as the person remembered'. He admits that although he finds the lyric 'I' an easy poetic technique, a prose 'I' proves much more difficult: 'it seems to be ... a process of revealing rather than concealment'. But private people don't lightly share truths about themselves, especially the truth of strong feeling and a friendship that was literally 'life-changing'.

Morgan himself should have the last word on public sharing, since what he says can apply to all our stories and relationships. Here are the remarkable closing stanzas of 'To the Librarians'. They provide an answer to the 'hard white whistle of existence' which has demanded to know why he is *not* averse to this stripping of the self:

> Why, there is no protection, I replied,
> What you have been and done's not set aside.
> Your files are you and file through one divide.
>
> Burn your letters, burn your boats: no tide
> will ever wash away the ash you hide
> of pain, or love, or pain or love denied.

Letter from Wales

Sam Adams

NOTE: *The dire situation of the National Library of Wales outlined in Sam Adams's 'Letter' in this issue has been mitigated by a Welsh Government announcement that fresh funding of £2.25 million will be made available for 2021 and 2022 'to safeguard jobs and deliver new strategic priorities'.*

When I was there in the early 1950s, Aberystwyth was bookended, west to east, by two grand buildings in contrasting styles. On the seafront was an odd jumble of Victorian Gothic, conceived as a railway hotel, the University College of Wales, and some 500 feet up on Penglais Hill overlooking the town, the 'great white stone building ... with an understated ... classical design' that is the National Library of Wales, or Nat Lib, as I shall always think of it. It is, and I quote again from the *Carmarthenshire and Ceredigion* volume of *The Buildings of Wales*, 'the most important cultural building in Wales'. Even today, Aberystwyth, more or less at the midpoint of the impressive bight of Cardigan Bay, is still fairly remote from the rest of Wales. Having travelled between Gilfach Goch and Aber as a student, by bus, I am allowed to testify to its remoteness, but I recall bridling at Christopher de Hamel's description of NLW in *Meetings with Remarkable Manuscripts* as 'one of the most magnificently inaccessible outposts of learning in the British Isles' (PNR 234), especially since the British Library and the Bodleian are at least as remote from my point of view. In those Aber years I spent little time at the National Library, even in postgraduate studies. It afforded me no more than I could obtain from or via the college library, which was a convenient short step from digs. (I should add, the unpublished Thomas Hood letters at Bristol Central Library levered me profitably out of my comfort zone.) In recent years, however, especially in my pursuit of T. J. Llewelyn Prichard, I have come to appreciate both the depth of resources and the inspired helpfulness of staff at the National Library, obtainable by email and the mere click of a mouse – and that, it turns out, is vital.

The National Library now shares Penglais Hill with the university campus. While not obscured by the hotchpotch of buildings above it, the site is certainly not 'lonely fair' as it once was. But the view from the library front on a clear day, out over the town to the great sweep of the bay embraced by the curves of the Llŷn peninsula to the north and the Pembrokeshire coast to the south, is still wonderful. I doubt a like institution anywhere in the world could surpass it. The library received its charter in March 1907. Professor Gwyn Jones was born the same year. This coincidence is worthy of mention because, on his death in 1999, the professor left his own substantial library, notably strong in seventeenth- and eighteenth-century literature and private-press books, to the National Library, where the collection is listed as 'Casgliad Castell Gwyn'. This follows the most worthy of ancient traditions: the philanthropy of bibliophiles. As is well known, great libraries have been built on 'foundation collections', the British Library notably on those of Sir Robert Cotton and Sir Hans Sloane, the Bodleian on those of Sir Thomas Bodley, and all he encouraged to follow suit. Sir John Williams (1840–1926), the *Dictionary of National Biography* tells us, was the principal founder of the National Library of Wales. The son of a Welsh Congregational minister and farmer (not an unusual combination), he was educated at a local school and then at the University of Glasgow and, after apprenticeship to a physician in Swansea, at University College Hospital, London. Having qualified MD, FRCP and begun medical practice in Swansea, he returned to London as a surgeon at University College Hospital. It was in Swansea he began collecting manuscripts, books and prints. He was involved with the 'Welsh Library Committee' at UCW, which set itself the target of creating both a national museum and a national library, the first in Cardiff and the second, at his insistence, in Aberystwyth. In 1898, the *Dictionary of National Biography* tells us, 'he purchased the "reversion" [the right to succeed to a property] of the magnificent Peniarth collection of manuscripts in Welsh, Latin, and other languages' with the intention of presenting it in due course to the National Library, which he was able to do in January 1909. He went on to give or bequeath all his books and manuscripts to the institution and a large sum of money. He became the library's first president, a post to which he was re-elected several times.

A press release of 30 September 2020 announced the publication of the first of a planned series of 'tailored' reviews of institutions sponsored by the Welsh government, based on a methodology suggested by the UK Cabinet Office. The privileged institution was the National Library. It has taken a few months for the implications of the review report to sink in and for the first rumours of or wild guesses at the Welsh government's response to slither out. The wildest of the latter suggest that the library will somehow be taken over by the British Library.

The number of visitors to NLW is decreasing, while the number of library *users* via the internet has increased remarkably. All major libraries are the same. Nevertheless, the report wants more visitors. In this respect it has a good deal of common sense to offer as well as some absurd tokenism, such as the Library should strive to become more welcoming to the youthful spirit of the age by providing a facility where visitors could have access to the web while eating, drinking and chatting together, the sort of facility apparently now available at the neighbouring university library, or an internet café. What is beyond question, and clearly seen by the review panel, is that the National Library of Wales has been underfunded for a decade. Its income has reduced from £9.97 million in 2007/8 to £9.6 million in 2018/19. In the same period staff numbers have reduced by more than a fifth, from 290 to 224. The review compares the Library's income with that of the National Library of Scotland, which in 2017/18 received £15.3 million, and the British Library, which in 2020/21 will scrape by on £97 million. Furthermore, NLW is entirely responsible for staff pensions, while the staff of Scotland's library and the British Library receive civil service pensions, to which the libraries contribute 20 percent.

While acknowledging that NLW 'has been at the forefront of developing digital skills and services for archives and libraries, in Wales *and internationally over the past decade, before the effects of austerity disrupted this work*' (my italics), the review recommends an increase in the scope of its activities in this field, in other kinds of 'outreach' programmes, and in links with other cultural institutions. All of the above requires increased staffing and funding at a time when the omens suggest further cuts are in the offing. As a user, I have nothing but admiration for Nat Lib and its staff. I have never been less than satisfied with the service it provides and can call to mind immediately several occasions when I have been, frankly, amazed at the ability of staff to respond to my vaguely framed requests. The solution to issues raised by the 'tailored review' panel lies with the Welsh government, which supplies about 93 percent of the Library's income. To simply kill off or sell off a national library would be an unconscionable act of vandalism that any government would shrink from, but many here believe the present Welsh government is in danger of inflicting 'death by a thousand cuts' on the primary repository of the principal expression of the culture of Wales.

Night Thoughts on *Night Thoughts*

John Clegg

In the 275 years since its publication, Edward Young's *Night Thoughts* has been praised, dispraised, and finally ignored, as a didactic poem, and a particularly heavy-handed specimen of the genre. J.R. Boyd, in the preface to his 1856 edition, recommended the poem for rote learning in schools, as 'furnish[ing] a great number of pithy sentences, easily remembered, and pregnant with the most important meaning, which, if lodged early in the mind, must exert a salutary influence' (and it goes on like this). If this is the best that can be said for it, it is obviously not likely to win many new readers today; I propose here a different approach to *Night Thoughts*.

Most eighteenth-century didactic poems cannot be read as dramatic monologues - that is, a form of poetry where the audience potentially knows more than the speaker. If we're not convinced by the argument in Cowper's 'Conversation', the poem falls apart, whereas Browning's 'My Last Duchess' fails if we *are* convinced (of the speaker's self-exoneration). *Night Thoughts* was certainly intended to be a poem of the first sort. It is much more convincing as a poem of the second, the furious thoughts of an elderly churchman in a chilly and draughty bedroom in Welwyn, as he begins to drift off to sleep.

These thoughts mostly concern 'Lorenzo', his imaginary twenty-something dissolute son (his real son, Frederick, was eight years old when the poem was published). They are sermons rather than arguments, but they refer back to arguments in the past between Young and Lorenzo - and here Young makes the decision, disastrous if he's writing a didactic poem but brilliant if he's writing a dramatic monologue, of repeating all of Lorenzo's jokes in order to rebut them. 'Thou sayst I *preach*; *Lorenzo!* 'tis confest; / What if, for once, I preach thee quite *awake*?' It is clear that Lorenzo doesn't take his father seriously; lying in bed, Young is trying to conjure into being the line which finally convinces him, but rounds, again and again, on the original attack. *Night Thoughts* is one of the great poems of *l'esprit de l'escalier*.

Of course if we've been hurt by a loved one we keep thinking about the precise words. Likewise, we are often unconsciously attuned to the weak spots in our own arguments. Night the Second is Young's furious attack on leisure: 'Blest leisure is our curse, like that of *Cain* / It makes us wander'. Children at play are an obvious counterexample: it would be hard to argue that they were being wicked. So, for his arguments' sake, Young should avoid mentioning children altogether; instead he brings them in constantly, whether or not they're wanted, in unnecessary metaphors:

> Like children babling nonsense in their sports,
> We censure nature for a span too short...

for instance, where the tenor of the metaphor is just 'speaking untruths'. 'The more our joy, the more we know it vain' is followed up by 'Who knows not this, tho' grey, is still a child'. Lorenzo's pleasures are 'rattles' or 'toys', a word Young brings into this Night again and again. 'Pregnant', likewise: 'Pregnant with all eternity can give, / Pregnant with all that makes arch-angels smile' - the only times the word is used in the poem - and metaphors from pregnancy: 'the man is yet unborn / Who duly weighs an hour'. Even God is figured, bizarrely, as a pregnant mother:

> That memorable hour of wond'rous birth,
> When the Dread Sire, on emanation bent,
> And big with nature, rising in his might,
> Call'd forth creation...

These metaphors from pregnancy and childhood do not recur in subsequent Nights. They are testament to the conflicted field Young's imagination is circling, made most vivid in Matthew 18 2-3: 'And Jesus called a little child unto him, and set him in the midst of them, | And said, Verily I say unto you, Except ye be converted, and become as little children, ye shall not enter into the kingdom of heaven'. The thoughts of Jesus on childishness are complex, hard to interpret; Young's didacticism is simple; the interest is in the way in which his imagination conspires against him.

I think this is even true for the detachable sentences praised by Boyd, the poem's only claim to have entered the language. 'Procrastination is the thief of time'; 'Tired nature's sweet restorer' (describing sleep); they are memorable enough that people quote them without knowing the source, they feel like the sort of thing which could be embroidered on samplers. But they are stranger than that, and stranger than Young meant them to be.

The central meaning of 'procrastination is the thief of time' is obviously that procrastination steals time, but the formation 'thief of' is unfamiliar (both today and in the eighteenth century); we are more likely to initially interpret the clause as 'thief belonging to time', which has its own weird, half-appropriate logic. Likewise, the idea that sleep restores 'tired nature' from tiredness, with 'nature' presumably meaning everything that sleeps, is a daft tautology - the earlier poets from whom Young borrowed his diction and vocabulary (especially Samuel Daniel) never came close to something so ridiculous. I suggest that the faintly woozy nature of the poem's best passages is almost deliberate: they have the exact feeling of 'sentences which seem profound when you're half-asleep'.

I can't pretend that all of *Night Thoughts* reads well when treated in this way; the Second, Fifth and Eighth nights work the best, the Sixth Night not at all. And in any case the poem is far too long. But I think back to the poor pupils of Dr Boyd mentioned in my first paragraph. If they read the poem for its insight into the world, its 'salutary influence', they must have been bored stiff. But if they read it for insight into their teacher...

Birds, Bugs, and a Ghost

From the Journals, 3 – 5 August 1995

R. F. Langley

On Holiday in the Old Meeting House, Wenhaston, Suffolk

To Blythburgh (*church*) in the afternoon, never more full of sun. The eleven angels, primed a little, maybe, by my watching dragonflies this morning, their hair flicked up, wings stretched and swept and pointed, up there in the shining with the eighteen windows either side framing intense summer blue and stamped with slanting diamond-leaded and thickened mullion. straw-coloured stone. The wall of the Portaloo in the bushes is too hot to lean on. I leave the rest drawing and reading and go down to the hide on the Angel Marshes. Blue and pink water runs in wavelets into green reeds and paler purslane, with drifts of sea lavender. The path through the reeds, over the slatted walkway, is almost choked, so you push through the harsh leaves, swishing. Its landward end is marked by climbing vetch, clumped to chest-high, in the shadow of trees, glowing purple, with humble-bees in it, an *agelena* web, and closed flowers of... is it a marsh sowthistle? Too small for that, but the colours are so insistent that they leave normal surfaces in space behind and float back into distance and out into the head.

Coming along the path I sat down on the edge several times to steady the binoculars in the cool wind. The tide is right in. Wavelets break rather at random, into small heads, fresh and alive. At least 500 lesser black-backed gulls tilt and dip, with small squads of black-headed at the edges of the flock. And, over the far side, pink... what has to be a flamingo, tall and only occasionally uncurling a neck. A Chilean flamingo, four people in the hide tell me. And they are watching a whimbrel, sleeping then preening and looking about, only a few yards away at the end of a spit of growth. Dark brown. Shortish, strong, down-curved black bill. Brown eye-stripe. Mottled cream and brown tail as it preens. The four people leave, with their mounted telescope. No one else comes. Oystercatchers and redshank in a frieze against a pale bank opposite. Ten or so cormorant on the stakes, some with wings held out. A heron on the far side, thin and stepping. Everything busy in the moving water and wind. Southwold dimmed and wriggling in heat. Blue sky running down to molten lead at its bottom.

In the evenings the swifts vanish... the low, charging parties in the day... the high zooming, spreading as we eat under the tree... then, what I didn't realise, they vanish up into the sky, above the reach of eyesight. A 'Nature Notes' in the *Guardian* tells me this... suggesting that they slant off and up until the thermals hold them... the writer never having managed to catch the moment of their rising, except on radar, over London, which showed the whole cloud of them lifting and dispersing. Tonight, B calls me into the garden to listen, and their calls are still audible though none of them are visible. We lie on our backs and look up into emptiness. The binoculars show nothing – except a column of weaving gnats above the cowl of the central chimney of our cottage, which connects, so far as I can see, to the empty hearth in the dining room. Maybe the metal cowl itself has soaked up and stored heat... it is a double chimney and the other pot, uncowled, has no gnats.

My evening walk up Wash Lane before dinner produces a smooth, streamlined mirid bug, uniform straw colour, long-antennaed and legged, black-eyed, somehow very simple and so very fundamental, on a furry-grass head... *Stenodema laevigatum* or something close. It is there when I come back an hour or more later, obviously settled for the night. It just turns round, head downward, and switches its antennae about. And a long-bodied, long-winged fly... with wings crossed by rows of black chequers, not perfectly aligned, and its tail, red, raised up between its wing tips... not in the book, I think, though very distinctive – black and white and red.

Walking back on this later trip I remember Mother seeing the woman crossing Hobs Hole Lane by the wood... then finding no footprints in the snow and no sign of her in the field... and feel how narrow this track is, with banks too choked and high to step aside if a woman came walking towards me out of the gloom... so I'm glad to hear the ping and pong of a shuttlecock behind the hedge and the voices of Eric and Ruth.

Friday evening. I watch the swifts over the garden and they finally vanish about ten minutes past nine, with darkness coming on and the clouds filling the sky, grey and level-bottomed, with melted combings of whiter ones between them and paled blue beyond. Suffusions of bone yellow. The birds were in a party of fifty or so, maybe not so many, but high for most of an hour, not getting higher. They moved gradually north over the village and their places were not taken by others. The rosy and golden sunset took place over Wash Lane... the swifts shrank, their voices just prickling the edge of silence; I could see them still with the binoculars, trembling, planing... but were they higher or just further away? I could not tell... then they had disappeared behind the trees surrounding the garden. A croak called my attention to two heron, rowing steadily southward. Small birds moved suddenly, very close in the hedge.

Edited by Barbara Langley, February 2021

Poems and Features

'Grodzinksi's Kosher Bakery' and Other Poems

MICHAEL BRETT

Tomorrow it will all run backwards

Tomorrow, it will all run backwards:

The steel tsunamis will froth back upwards
And become solid again.
The planes will be pulled out like javelins
And slide backwards, swallowing their vapour trails.

Tomorrow, everyone will be fine.

Tomorrow, everyone who died will come home.
They will sit again at the tables of home
And rejoin life's fellowship, its snapshots
And picnics.

Tomorrow, all will be well.

It will be as if it all never happened.
Everyone will sleep as babies do under mobiles,
Untroubled by strange sounds, of aero engines
Flying too low and shadows cast over the streets.

Tomorrow, mobile phones will just be toys again.

The Return of Sparrowhawks to Battersea Power Station

High on a power-station chimney top,
Aloof in a nest and always hungry,
Imagine the city as a sparrowhawk sees it:

The surrounding clouds, pale and thin as ribs in sand;
The tube trains clattering like spoons,
The plane wings like steel knives and forks,
Over the city.

Wings spread like concertinas, they fall, then fly
To drift on light rumours of a breeze
Reviewing – with cool fighter pilot's eyes –
The estuary mouth, the metropolis gulping reservoirs;
The beef-gut diagram of the uncoiled Thames

High over the globe; high over the Hammersmith flyover,
They tilt their wings, indifferent to the streams of words and cars.

To their infrared, in the bright maze of the streets below
Each rat glows like a burning coal.
They are camera guns focusing to single points,
Ransacking all of London with their eyes.

On Easdale Island

On Easdale island, the rain is bilingual but
The wind speaks Gaelic and the sea speaks English, but
The faces in the scree and cliffs are always silent.

Sometimes, like imagined Easter Island heads, I can see entire families, with eyes of moss
Staring over the flooded quarries, each one an oblong pool of water, on its back
As if lounging on a beach towel, each casually
Reviewing the surgeon Moon at the black Atlantic's bedside.

Sometimes, like a dying man, the hissing sea breathes aloud,
Recalls its greatness; thinks of the thousands made to wave goodbye;
Or turns in its bed and sees
The entrance to the Firth of Lorn, with its remains
Of beached, torpedoed ships; where
The hooligan sea stops thumping in the shallower water,
And – pointing its waves – makes a scholarly demonstration
Of parallelograms; of every trapezium in giant and rusting steel
From vanished shipyards.

Above them, in the muttering cliffs, imagined faces in granite albums pass one another
Impossible and dangerous bouquets of stunted trees,
Wedged in gaps more impossible than chance; ones that threaten too
A final midnight plunge, like King Alexander's horse in
Geological storms of flying kings
And families waving, waving from one-way ships.

Grodzinksi's Kosher Bakery

Coiled in the ammonite darkness, we never see the future
But confuse it with rumours and predictions
Of Thunderbirds Tracy Island
And cheap holidays on the moon.

Look. Here is survival. Marc Bolan ate here
In the Manor House kosher bakery. Around us, like gentle waves,
The ultra-orthodox slide the bread across the glass counter
Which reflects their faces upside down.
The hats, the shtreimels, like sci-fi flying saucers, converge
Both in Yiddish and in English.

A pretty, young black woman, with a baby in a pushchair,
Passing by outside, hardly glances at the busy lunchtime trade;
Or the Yiddish writing, like the marks of birds' feet on a kind of beach
Where survivors of European shipwrecks nest and thrive.

Shafts of light, black coats and stacks of bread converge in columns
Like a backwards look at Futurism in the Tate.
A kind of joy weaves together with the voices and the bread,
On a safe and final island
Where the London bus turns left to Stamford Hill.

The future was never to be a holiday on the moon,
And the buzzing in the earth we hear
Is not miners' drills, but inside a kind of amber,
Where a giant dragonfly is not dead but still alive.

The Crab Nebula Tea Detectives

Each mile in the universe is a longing for more tea.
We are the Crab Nebula Tea Detectives. We rummage in stellar constellations
For teas in other worlds, on other planets.
We have found tea in the Crab Nebula exhaling purple gas;
London blend Darjeeling Tea in clouds longer, straighter than the Jurassic or Cretaceous ages.
Constellations, clouds of English Breakfast Tea both conceal and reveal mystery,
Like a lover's shoes behind bedroom curtains;
But the Crab Nebula cluster conceals both the directness of the burglar and the honesty of Tea
Outside the Van Allen Belt, among the meteors, the satellites chirping in digital codes.

Old Tea Detectives never die, we name stars after them
In Constellations Dad and Auntie.
That way, we can see and drink with them forever,
Not like mugshots at the station,
But in a private gallery, high and over us in star clusters
Like golden picture frames. We are never alone if we look up,
During a gun fight or a car chase over tea.
Our religious denomination is Darjeeling, hot brown tea.
It is stronger than snow, stronger than official stamps.
It steams in every Universe. It lifts Schrödinger cats from armchairs
And firemen out of trees.

Tea is the eternal primal substance of the Universe.
It burns yellow inside all Suns and in all souls.
It drives power plants. It drives the worm. It grows black inside the coal mines,
In false beards and honest disguises. The bullet that flutters like a butterfly
Towards the sunlit body armour sings itself to sleep as it dreams
Of Darjeeling, and of PG Tips in bags. In supermarkets,
Boxes of biscuits sing like Cambridge choirs to the teabags,
Each one dancing, like Nijinsky, to the sounds of kettles, to the dance of spoons
Pirouetting inside cups. Their Assam and their dunking
Curves around the Rings of Saturn in the Time and Space Continuum.

Our Quantum Teas are each a quantum ballerina spinning,
Inside each and every Sun, untouched by Time's decay, or even the smallest changes.
They are both remote and far, Einsteinian in complexity and simplicity.
The wonders and the truths of tea ride like surfboards on wave crests, faster than light,
Faster than steam. They arrive before they leave.

That is the mystery of the Universe: its dimensions like cakes, the sandwich-pink streaks
Of Jupiter and the blue, forgotten sardine depths of Pluto; each colour longing, stretching
Itself towards the little match-flame Sun, millions of miles away;
Each mile in the Universe is a longing for more tea.

Bodiam Castle

The castle guards nothing now but summer:
Standing knee-deep in its moat, silent, like a fisherman
Among its lily pads, its frogs, its willow trees
And buzzing biplane dragonflies.

Through the yellow oblong arrow slits and doorless doorways
You can see them all, like impressionist paintings,
The flowers and the fish ruffling the ancestral lace
At the throat of evening.

This afternoon, the helmet, the longbow
And the hands that fed them were lost, forgotten
Like the pollen of petrified forests;
Like swords in a lake.

But tonight, look down from the tower at the headlights:
The army convoys wink and are gone
And – above us – fighter jets like Bolsheviks in a Russian palace
Leave snowy footprints in the corridor air;

And everything that seemed so straight, so true,
Was just the prelude to some imperial theme
Where a triumphant Othello kills not just his wife.

Vienna

Marius Kociejowski

A green Tyrolean hat with a feather tucked in its side was the reason I swore never to go back to Vienna. Also there had been the man at the cash till in the shop of the Kunsthistorisches Museum who, when I bought some postcards, took each one and slowly bent it, not so much that it would cause a crease but enough to indicate his opinion of me while at the same time putting himself just beyond the reach of accusation. Pettiness is the functionary's most finely honed weapon and against it there is very little by way of defence except, perhaps, pretending not to notice. I rack my brain for a likeness of him, a single detail, a broken button or an unruly eyelash, anything to give him a voice, a presence, but it was all such a long time ago and, if my calculations are correct, the silly fool is in his grave. Why, though, this ridiculous exercise of power? Did he not, as I do, have to bow down to tie his shoelaces? Are we not, by this act alone, made humble?

Another reason for my intense dislike of Vienna was that not a single B&B would give us a bed for the night, every enquiry we made met with a sharp *nein* even when rooms were advertised as available. It was almost as if there were some network of spies, warning people in advance of a suspicious, roving couple. It would be the same story, a day later, in Salzburg where finally we got a room in a small hotel owned by an Italian couple. These are the only times in my life I've been refused a room. Admittedly, I cut a somewhat barbaric figure in 1974 Vienna, still one of the most conservative cities in Europe. I had long hair and wore a black leather jacket, and, maybe the most incongruous detail in an already doubtful profile, I travelled with a portable typewriter. Surely I was up to no good. I was. My verses were execrable. At about midnight, with nowhere to stay, we were rescued by a couple of students from London who let us sleep on their floor. One day in Vienna was enough for me.

I did like the *ancien régime* cafés.

Something I'd learned earlier that day seemed to epitomise the city and its people for me. One of the two architects of the Wiener Staatsoper, whose name I now discover was Eduard van der Nüll, committed suicide in 1868 when, unbeknownst to him, revised plans for the Ringstrasse saw to it that the boulevard in front of the opera house was elevated by a metre, thereby cancelling out the front ramp going up to the main entrance. It was a classic case of like minds not sitting at the same table. Among the jibes the architects had to endure was that the opera house was now, in addition to being insufficiently grand, a 'sunken chest' or, worse still, 'the Königgrätz of Construction', Königgrätz being the town closest to where the Austrian army was routed by a much smaller Prussian army a couple of years earlier. Among the mockers was the emperor himself, Franz Joseph I, who I picture twirling his friendly mutton chops. Should the unfortunate Eduard van der Nüll be made to stand in for the Viennese? I was not yet of an age to be able to distinguish between the fool and the man of honour or to appreciate the fact they are often one and the same. Quite simply, I took him for a stiff neck, which was how many of the older Viennese struck me. Something else I now discover, which ought not to make a difference but maybe it does, is that architects Eduard van der Nüll and August Sicard von Sicardsburg as well as being business partners were also a couple. So how did that wash with the more starched elements of Viennese society? Was it not enough that the emperor's younger brother, Archduke Ludwig Viktor, 'Luziwuzi' as he was known by friends and foes alike, had his marsupial features slapped after he made an inopportune advance towards an officer in the city's famous bathhouse? Might it be that the scorn poured over Eduard van der Nüll and August Sicard von Sicardsburg was silently augmented with prejudice? We will probably never know for sure because in deeply conservative circles a veil tends to fall over the unspeakable. What we do know is that Franz Joseph felt badly about Eduard van der Nüll's suicide and never again slung mud at anyone. From then on, each new enterprise was greeted with the formulaic sentence: '*Es war sehr schön, es hat mich sehr gefreut.*' ('It was very nice,' he'd say, 'I was very pleased.') A polite though ultimately meaningless remark, it is the one by which he is best remembered and it's even the title of a book about him. I had little time for the emperor or his empire, the jaunty militarism and the cheery *Militärmusik* that accompanied it, but when years later I read Joseph Roth's *The Radetzky March* with its unforgettable portrait of the emperor in his dotage I realised there was more to him and more to the Austro-Hungarian Empire than a callow youth could understand. And who cannot at the very least pause and consider what Roth, an author I revere, loved? As for the architectonic couple it is not unreasonable to suppose the death of one hastened the death of the other. August Sicard von Sicardsburg died six weeks later, from tuberculosis according to the death certificate, but surely it was more than that. Surely heartbreak came into it. If things are often more complex than the words used to describe them, it's because the greater part of love belongs to silence.

The tipping point for me came when we took the train from Vienna to Salzburg. A man in his seventies wearing a green Tyrolean hat and a moss-green coat of loden cloth with a long pleat down the back stepped into our compartment and although he had nothing with him motioned to me to clear a space on the luggage rack above him. Our bags were bulky and there was my typewriter too. The man studied my labours with a beady eye before insisting I had not yet allowed him his equal share of space. After I made further adjustments, the man, satisfied that justice had been done, very slowly removed his green Tyrolean hat with the side feather and placed it on the middle of the rack. When he got off at the next stop, I swore then never to go back to Vienna.

Forty-five years later, I returned, bearing the sword of vengeance, ready to lay waste to its populace or at least those wearing green Tyrolean hats and moss-green coats of loden cloth, the uniform, so it seemed to me, of men old enough to have been alive during the war and who were still suffering from a deep sense of victimhood as if the Anschluss, the union of Austria and Nazi Germany, had nothing to do with them. Vienna in 1974 was a city of the old and now, in 2019, it was a city of the young, although in truth it was I who'd aged and those who were old then are old no more. They've become death's spring chickens. I was to be frustrated in my murderous scheme. Almost immediately, I was disarmed by several instances of charm and grace.

*

My reason for going back was to attend the American composer Michael Hersch's epic three-part cycle *Sew Me into a Shroud of Leaves*. It was scheduled to begin at five in the morning. Yes, I too had to read that several times. Could this be a first in the history of musical performance? The concert, including intervals, was to cover a period of fifteen hours, twelve of them dedicated to some of the most absolute music of our time. I was determined to stick it out from beginning to end, bring to it my own sense of the absolute. My wife, though willing, was not prepared to lose sleep and would join me later. Wanting to be sure I'd be able to get to where I believed the concert would be, the Wiener Konzerthaus, and how I would get there from where we were staying, I went into tourist information and there spoke to a woman who resembled a willow tree. (There are such women, women who are like willow trees, a rare quality, but instantly recognisable.) Brigitte Nemeth gave me directions to the Wien Konzerthaus and when she expressed surprise at the early start I told her about Michael Hersch and offered the information that the composition of the third and lengthiest part of the work I had come to hear was based on his reading of my poetry. I suggested she join us, but she said she had to work. When I said that maybe modern classical music was not to her liking she spoke of how when listening to it at home it remains remote but that when hearing it live, the physical fact of being there helps to resolve one's difficulties with it. She confirmed for me what I already knew; the major difference between recorded and live music is that with the first we listen to it primarily with our minds, the second with our whole bodies. If cities can be said to have a resident muse, she was it.

The next morning, at 4.45 – it was raining – I found myself hammering on the darkened entrance of the Wiener Konzerthaus on Lothringerstraße. When nobody stirred inside, I walked around the building looking for a rear entrance. There was nobody about at that hour, and so, with there being nothing more I could do, I walked to a nearby hotel where I was treated to another instance of Viennese hospitality. The night porter checked his computer for information and, finding the concert was not at the Konzerthaus but at the Österreichische Nationalbibliothek, put me in a cab there. The driver remarked laconically that he didn't think it was open yet and I just as laconically said I understood it was. I was half an hour late. At the marble entrance I could hear familiar violent chords being struck in the distance. When the first interval arrived an excited woman came up to me, saying that Brigitte Nemeth had contacted her to say she had given me directions to the wrong place and that both she and her colleague, Ingrid Woelfl, had searched the whole of Vienna for me, phoning hotels and B&Bs. They even got in touch with the artistic director of Wien Modern, asking him to get in touch with Michael Hersch who might know of our whereabouts. We had domiciled ourselves beneath the radar, a rather bleak room in the working-class Meidling district which has its own dialect and a museum, the only one in Europe devoted to heating systems.

Sew Me into a Shroud of Leaves comprises *The Vanishing Pavilions*, a piano sonata in fifty movements, which the composer based on his reading of the poetry of our mutual friend Christopher Middleton; *Last Autumn*, a fairly rare combination of French horn and cello, which draws on W. G. Sebald's 'prose poem' *After Nature*; and, as previously mentioned, the première of *one day may become menace*, a massive work of sixty-two movements for piano, spanning six hours. There is no greater tribute for a poet than for a composer to take from his work something for his own purpose. The others can keep their gaudy prizes. I have written elsewhere on Hersch's music, and so, to briefly summarise, the composer takes his cue not from entire poems but from fragments – single lines or even phrases from lines and, just occasionally, short passages – which in themselves may have little meaning for the casual reader but which for him are the ignition points for his most inventive musical passages, the poetic fragment as delectable to him as are church ruins to believers and unbelievers alike.

Almost the entirety of Hersch's musical output is a depiction of annihilation and putrescence. I remember Christopher Middleton saying to me once, 'I can't work out what goes on in that young man's head.' So why did Christopher, who normally preferred the efflorescence of the 'Les Six', so admire him? And why do I, when so much new music leaves me cold? The answer in both instances, Christopher's and mine, is that in Hersch's music there is a struggle between the lyrical and a world in which the lyrical is no longer possible or even allowable. The music builds and demolishes, it builds and demolishes. Countless are the times when several notes in a row threaten to become hummable and then, just in time, there comes a cascade of aural violence. Small wonder one of his early pieces is called *the wreckage of flowers*, its title a perfect illustration of what he does. This struggle makes him one of the most compelling voices in the present musical landscape, but it is a form of genius that resides in a particular dark groove and I wonder if there is anything on earth that will make him shift to a position more celebratory of life. The danger in doing so is that it might become pastiche, an empty expression of reassurance.

The closest parallel I've found in the visual arts is in the devastated landscapes of Anselm Kiefer. What I admire in the one, I find in the other. They are two artists of our time with whom a reckoning will have to be made. Certainly, both are poetry-driven and both have a fascination with fragments or remnants, worlds on the cusp of disappearance. I have looked at Kiefer's work and *heard* it; I have listened to Hersch and *seen* it. I would say Hersch's vision is the bleaker of the two. When he was close to completing *one day may become menace* he wrote to me, asking whether I'd be prepared to write several lines on the theme of bodily putrefaction, upon which he might conclude his work. I refused. My poetry may be dark and it may be deeply pessimistic in nature, but never does it subscribe to the luxury of intellectual despair. I am not suggesting Hersch luxuriates, far from it, but I wonder if dissolution has become a bit of a habit with him, which sooner or later he'll have to break if he's to move forward. This aside, I don't question his integrity for a minute.

The artistic director of the Wien Modern, Bernhard Günther, who with his ponytail looked as though he just stepped out of *Così Fan Tutte*, when faced with the problem of how to accommodate the enormous canvas of Hersch's cycle and how an audience could be expected to sit through twelve hours of music, spent several months searching for a solution and finally settled on the Prunksaal, the State Hall of the Austrian National Library (Österreichische Nationalbibliothek). A jewel of the Baroque, its domed ceiling covered with frescos, and at the centre of its marbled floor Antonio Corradini's marble statue of the library's founder, Emperor Charles VI got up as Hercules of the Muses, it was, he realised, the ideal place. A library, Günther told me, is one of the few places where people behave with utmost consideration, and the Prunksaal is so designed that it would allow for people to come and go as they like without too much distraction. A perfectionist, he arranged even for the distribution of blankets and mattresses. At the same time he managed to bring a potentially distant and highly challenging work into an intimate sphere. The musicians were placed directly beneath the high dome, which had the visual and aural effect of isolating them in a huge space. As much a metaphysician as he is an organiser, Günther harnessed the heavens. The music began in darkness and, in keeping with the progression of the music, moved from artificial to natural light and finally, with the concert ending at eight in the evening, darkness again. Stephanie Fleischmann, the librettist for Hersch's opera *Poppaea*, said of the Prunksaal that it was 'the perfect stage design for a piece about a perished culture'. She put into words precisely what first drew me to his music, a sense of it being the surviving remnants of some lost civilisation.

A total work of art, or what in German is called *Gesamtkunstwerk*, the baroque splendour of the Prunksaal is, as with so much else in Vienna, tainted by recent history. After the Anschluss its librarian, Josef Bick, was imprisoned and replaced with Paul Heigl, a fervent member of the Schutzstaffel, better known as the SS, who pursued a policy of seizing the libraries of prominent Jewish individuals, which included the magnificent collection of Alphonse Mayer von Rothschild. A good Nazi to the end, Heigl, together with his wife, took an overdose of sleeping pills in 1945. Bick was reinstated. The problem he and his successors had to face was what to do with the 50,000 volumes that had been confiscated from Jewish families, a process of reparation that is still underway. Would it be stating the obvious to suggest that the presence of Michael Hersch's music in this of all places was a form of justice?

And so what did I make of *one day may become menace*? And was it illustrative of my work? The answer to the first question is that I was too curious to be able to judge of it. That would come later and, as with so many of Hersch's works, it would slowly ripen in my affections. I had been dropped into a sonic landscape with neither map nor compass, and without any musical language to describe it. What I can say is that from beginning to end I was taken by it, swept from movement to movement as if by a strong undertow. One could easily drown in its complexities. As to whether it was illustrative it hardly matters because, after all, the illustrative is merely *illustrative*. I wasn't looking for, or expecting, echoes of my own voice. What mattered was whether whatever the composer took from me was fully realised on his own terms because only then would it be a truly creative response. It was. And as such it was all I could have wished for. This is not to say I was not presented with difficulties. There is no getting round the fact that Hersch's music is not easy listening, but even so I found myself in a dreamlike state. I did not fidget, I did not yawn. I was alert even in my somnambulism, maybe even more so. I was curious as to how such a massive work could be resolved. I was to be greatly surprised. The concluding movement, which is a recapitulation of various themes scattered throughout the work, takes its cue from 'The Polar Bear', a poem that has been noted for its tenderness, which I accept, but what is rarely remarked is its underlying sense of menace. A father observes his infant daughter asleep in her cradle. The world outside is full of turbulence. It shakes the bedroom window in its embrasure. It is a poem as much about terror as it is about love. 'I listen to your small breathing. / My daughter, I seek a connection / Between all this: these are distances / The stammering mind cannot hold.' And it was there in the music. Michael Hersch 'got' it. What he'd earlier sought from me was inapplicable.

While I may be serious in wishing to take a work of music wholly on its own terms, I'm not immune to interference, the intrusion of things quite outside what the music expresses. I can't listen to the beginning of Shostakovich's String Quartet No. 5 without seeing a couple of Central Asian horsemen galloping over a vast plain, a mauve band of mountains in the distance. The pianist Jacob Rhodebeck seemed to be possessed of ... supernatural powers, as fresh five hours into the performance as he was at the beginning of it, and when he performed one of the more explosive movements, which draws on the lines in my poem 'Shrubland' ('A hieroglyph of broken twigs, / The skeletons of small animals, / The sticking burr of thistle'), suddenly, quite unbidden, there came to me a memory of the composer from the year before.

22 June 2018. We were at Aldeburgh where the evening before we had attended the première of Hersch's work for two soprano voices and chamber ensemble, *I hope we get a chance to visit soon*, a musical elegy for two women, the poet Rebecca Elson and the other a close friend of his, Mary Harris O'Reilly, both of whom died of cancer. Step by step the physical decline of both women is rendered in their own words, often in the most excruciating detail. Normally, I can swallow darkness whole, but this was too much for me. Later, I argued with Hersch, saying that the purpose of music, if not in fact all art, is to rise above the condition of our corruptible bodies. I cited Beethoven's *String Quartet in A minor*. Michael, from his side, declared it was the duty of an artist to tell the truth, however unpalatable it may be. Our failure to meet on this issue was, and continues to be, counterbalanced by mutual respect and profound friendship. Whether he gets a small or sizable audience is of virtually no consequence for him, any contemplation of whether the response is positive or negative borders on bad taste, and, if presented with an opportunity to win an audience, as was the case in Aldeburgh, it is just as likely that he will go at it with a battering ram, not because he seeks shock and awe but because, again, what has to be has to be. It makes him at once one of the most admirable and exasperating of composers.

The following morning, Hersch, the soprano Ah Young Hong, my wife and I went for a walk along the seemingly endless shingle beach, which, together with the fish and chips, is one of Aldeburgh's most celebrated features. It was fast approaching noon and as yet Hersch had had nothing to eat or drink, which confirmed what I have long suspected, that his metabolism is not that of ordinary mortals. He hungered for, and yet could not bring himself to order, fish and chips. An inability to decide on the things of this world is one of his more extraordinary characteristics, given that creatively he is one of the most resolute of people. He wanted first to go for a walk. We went along the beach to where stood Maggi Hambling's sculptural monument to Benjamin Britten, a couple of interlocking scallop shells, the bigger one with letters cut into the rim which read I HEAR THOSE VOICES THAT WILL NOT BE DROWNED, words taken from Humphrey Slater's libretto for Britten's opera *Peter Grimes*. A thing not offensive in itself, it would have been better placed in the town centre, a small distance away from what it seeks to evoke. Would one place in the middle of a forest the statue of a tree? So why a scallop on the seashore?

We began to collect pebbles. The best pebbles are widely considered to be those that have a pleasingly symmetrical shape, and I suppose people can be divided into those who love round ones and those who, such as myself, prefer the flattened ovoid pebbles that are a solid black, brown or white, or, more rarely, with a hint of translucence. My wife is an inveterate gatherer of pebbles and in common with the most discriminating collectors takes no more than two or three at a time. I found a pale one shaped like a small bird's egg, which I gave to Ah Young as a keepsake. I hope she has it still. Michael seemed to be fascinated by the whole business and started collecting pebbles as well, a little timidly as if this were his first time. I would never have marked him for a connoisseur of pebbles, but maybe with the more symmetrical ones he sees in them musical qualities.

Suddenly, and this is what came back to me in the Prunksaal, the air was full of thrips, also known as storm flies, thunder flies, thunder blights, thunderbugs, storm bugs, corn flies, corn lice and harvest flies. The storm imagery associated with many of the names relates to the folkloric belief that they are an augur of thunderstorms. Attached to this is the as yet unproven hypothesis that their big moment comes when the earth is negatively and the atmosphere positively charged. Astonishingly, there are approximately 6,000 different varieties of thrips and, whichever one it was that descended upon the beach at Aldeburgh, there were millions of them, which may be why the word 'thrips' covers both the singular and plural forms. A single thrips is difficult to imagine. They got into everything, our hair, our eyes, our clothes, the more adventurous of them making it as far as our underwear. The beach was sloped in shelves and Hersch, who had become separated from us, perhaps lost in the contemplation of his pebbles, was a level or two above where we were. Suddenly, he broke into a run, which is not easily done on a shingle beach where the pebbles slip and slide with every step one takes. The man seen in profile, frantically beating the air about himself, was no longer Michael Hersch the composer, nor was he Michael Hersch my friend, but the sole representative of our species, a man alone in the universe, the missing element of some immense metaphysical puzzle we'll never be able to solve, and now, in the baroque confines of the Prunksaal, those thrips had become musical notations filling the lines of the stave.

I noticed a woman in the front row, bunched up against the growing chill, wearing a leopard-skin-patterned coat, her head buried inside a woollen orange toque, and beside her a pair of bright red crutches. She seemed to me a cross between a figure in a painting by Pieter Brueghel the Younger and the amorphic 'Old Guy' one sees on Guy Fawkes Night. Suddenly, in the middle of Movement XXXVII, which in my notes I describe as funereal, she rose and, supporting herself on crutches, walked in the mechanical manner of those who are crippled as opposed to merely lame, the extraordinary thing being that she moved in perfect time to the music. A few minutes later, she returned, again walking in perfect time. I knew then I had to find out who she was. When the interval came I snuck up behind her at the bar and when she ordered a glass of red wine I cut in and bought it for her. We fell into conversation. Sylvia Wagner-Weger is a conceptual artist. I have since looked for her work or such as can be found on the internet and from the few things I've seen I am unable to judge of their merit, and, as is so often the case, the language used to describe what she does rather than illuminate obfuscates. What I read about her work is that she uses household materials such as sponge cloths to order to address 'the hidden mechanisms of power and oppression in the domestic environment', which doesn't particularly enlighten me. What I greatly like, on the other hand, are the words she herself uses, which serve as a kind of manifesto: *Was ist, war. Was war, ist.* (What is, was. What was, is.) She told me her output and opportunities to exhibit had been sharply reduced in recent years with the onset of multiple sclerosis. So that's what it was. I'd seen that mechanical birdlike movement before. I could not but admire the courage with which she faces her growing immobility. She said she would sooner walk on crutches than submit to the wheelchair. And I complimented her on her willpower at which she started laughing.

'Wheel power,' she cried, 'wheel power! I love it!'

After the concert Bernhard Günther took Hersch and his retinue to a restaurant on the very outskirts of Vienna, much of it still countryside. This was no idle choice. The winery of Mayer am Pfarrplatz had been a health spa in earlier times and it was there, in 1802, that Beethoven took a rest cure and wrote the heart-rending letter now referred to as the 'Heiligenstädter Testament' in which he relates the spiritual agony brought on by his loss of hearing: 'Ah, how could I possibly admit an infirmity in the one sense which ought to be more perfect in me than others, a sense which I once possessed in the highest perfection, a perfection such as few in my profession enjoy or ever have enjoyed.' Although the letter was ostensibly addressed to his brothers, it was never sent and in all probability was never meant to be. Mayer am Pfarrplatz was an extraordinary place to be, although it was a shade Teutonically cute.

The pianist Jacob Rhodebeck sat beside me, and sitting opposite was Jessica Lustig who some years before had been the first person to publish Hersch's music. I made a bit of sport with her. She is a theatrical as well as a musical agent and so I told her, in a somewhat pleading voice, that I had a play she might like, which I'd been working on for several decades. I've never written a play in my life. I watched with wicked glee as she hastily moved into defensive mode. Our talk turned to the performance. Jessica Lustig and Jacob Rhodebeck agreed that the work ended on a note of total despair. This troubled me. As if stuck inside some posthumous existence, where I could eavesdrop upon but not actually join other people's conversation, I said nothing, unable, just then, to communicate my disagreement. My venison dumplings sat heavily on their bed of red cabbage. Hersch was at the far end of the lengthy table, too far away for me to be able to get his thoughts on the matter. A year later, when finally I got to converse with him over the ending of *one day may become menace*, he would not be drawn one way or the other.

'Menace is certainly distinct from despair I would think, although when one considers the unenviable state of being under threat it could bring one to despair,' he replied. 'To be honest, I'm not happy with any of the characterisations, as I'm not even sure what it was that I felt at the end of that journey. Something, certainly. But what, I don't think I could peg down.'

This was good enough for me, who dwells in Keats's realm of uncertainties.

*

A couple of weeks prior to going to Vienna, I was shown on a computer screen a darkened area of my brain through which no thought will ever again enter or leave. There could be no telling what I'd lost as there was no telling what I had in the first place. Maybe I had been disburdened of bad memories although my dreams or at least what I can remember of them are much as they've always been, unless, of course, they've become worse. Apparently, though, the brain runs its own compensation scheme and what's lost in one place resurfaces in another. As I was still undergoing tests, one for the attractively named pulsus bisferiens, I did not dare ask whether it was advisable to travel for fear the answer would be no. I subscribe to a certain amount of disobedience. What I took to Vienna with me was a recharged sense of my own mortality, a small dose of which serves not only as some kind of corrective, but also as a spur to deeper feeling. One wouldn't wish for more as more might be a lethal dose. It was in Vienna that I would suffer – no, 'suffer' is the wrong word entirely – I would *experience* my first instance of Stendhal syndrome. Whether this was a direct consequence of my earlier problem, I don't know, and in fact, I'm not sure whether there really is such a thing as Stendhal syndrome. These days any excess of feeling calls for a purgative.

The term was coined in 1979 by the Italian psychiatrist Graziella Magherini who noticed the high incidence of tourists becoming mentally and physically overwhelmed in her native Florence. It is hard not to be when in Florence. I remember being in the Uffizi Gallery in a small room that had on one wall Titian's *Venus of Urbino*, surely one of the most erotic paintings in existence, and, on the adjacent wall, Leonardo da Vinci's *Annunciation*, one of the most spiritual. I hear that like naughty children they have been put into separate rooms. Sacred and profane thus entwined was almost too much for me. The clinical definitions of Stendhal syndrome leave something to be desired. It is most commonly described as a psychosomatic response to a beautiful work of art, which includes tachycardia (quite possible in my case), vertigo (which, if it means being knocked off-kilter, maybe), fainting (no smelling salts were required), confusion (only if confusion is on a par with revelation) and hallucination (in which case, if it requires imagination to see things as they are, then, yes, I hallucinated what was there right in front of me). If all this adds up to a psychosomatic disorder then it is no less than what any artist would like to see his work induce in other people. At the risk of moving into an aery dimension, I would describe it as a seizure of the soul. The soul, however, has been served notice, and what we have in its place, so claim the neuroscientists, is a series of complex chemical reactions that at the point of death cease. If so, then I and billions of others have been deluded and God's filling out forms at the unemployment office. Why do nurses the world over still open the windows in the rooms where people have just died? It is so their souls might escape. I subscribe to what someone has called 'quantum weirdness', which is a friendly phrase for the unknowable. Also I've got a sneaky feeling when the soul departs the body it regenerates as birdsong, its wavelength spanning a squawk and a trill.

Say, then, it really was a seizure of the soul, would that chronically unreliable genius, Marie-Henri Beyle, otherwise known as Stendhal, agree? Stendhal got *his* bout of Stendhal syndrome in Florence, in the Basilica of Santa Croce, but then he describes it in terms closer to what I experienced than anything I've found in my brief survey of clinical studies: 'I was in a sort of ecstasy,' he writes, 'from the idea of being in Florence, close to the great men whose tombs I had seen. Absorbed in the contemplation of sublime beauty ... I reached the point where one encounters celestial sensations ... Everything spoke so vividly to my soul. Ah, if I could only forget. I had palpitations of the heart, what in Berlin they call "nerves". Life was drained from me. I walked with the fear of falling.' *Ah, if I could only forget* – I don't quite believe Stendhal when he says this. What would *dottoressa* Magherini say to my having been shanghaied not in Florence but in Vienna?

So what did it for me? At the Kunsthistorisches Museum, scene of my old annoyance, I saw the Caravaggio/Bernini exhibition; an exquisite, small ninth-century Carolingian ivory relief, originally a book cover, of Pope Gregory writing at his desk, a dove representing the Holy Ghost whispering into his ear; Titian's portrait of Isabella d'Este as a very young woman, a girl almost, in a wonderful balzo headdress, although I now learn she was sixty-two when Titian painted her and already a bit on the stout side; several Breughels that took me back to childhood when I'd spend hours lying on the floor, studying the details in quarto-sized volume issued by the Metropolitan Museum of Art; and, Titian again, his *Woman in a Fur Coat*, who, I'm delighted to discover, is the very same who modelled for his *Venus of Urbino*. It was something altogether more modest that floored me, a marble female bust described as an ideal portrait of Petrarch's Laura by the Dalmatian artist Francesco Laurana (1430–1502) or, to those Croats who wish to claim him as their own, Frane Vranjanin. It is one of only nine such works by him, which are widely remarked for their beautiful, geometrically simple, faces. There is another in Palermo, which I saw some years ago. This one has the look of a girl who is not about to respond to the rude taunts being made by her fellow classmates, some of whom will think her bit snooty whereas really she is above the world's cares. This is what Petrarch says about her: *'Non era l'andar suo cosa mortale / ma d'angelica forma'*, or, in Anthony Mortimer's excellent translation, 'She moved not like a mortal, but as though / she bore an angel's form'. Angels can take all that you throw at them and more. Laurana took extra care with this sculpture, adding coloured wax to bring out her features, and, now missing, put a real jewel above her forehead where there had been a decorative *ferronnière* such as women wore during the Renaissance. The catalogue claims it may in fact be a portrait of Ippolita Maria Sforza, the first wife of Alfonso, Duke of Calabria, but there is already a bust of her by Laurana and it does not strike me as the same woman. It also says it might be Ippolita's daughter, Isabella, but I see little resemblance between this and an early engraving of her in which a double chin is quite pronounced. The claim to this being Petrarch's Laura is not wholly unfounded as it is quite possible Laurana saw the colour life drawing of Laure de Noves, in the Biblioteca Medicea Laurenziana, in Florence. She is a strong candidate for the woman who inspired Petrarch's verses. The historical evidence for Petrarch's Laura is meagre, and even during his lifetime there were those who thought she was merely a figment of his imagination. The poet in one of his letters scoffs at the suggestion: *'Simulatio esset utinam et non furor!'* ('Could such a fiction have continued for so long!') I see no reason to suppose he was not a fool for love. Also it is the delicious pain the man of feeling conjures for himself in order to keep the Muse close. It has been suggested that Giorgione's *Laura*, also in the Kunsthistorisches, might be a portrait of Laure de Noves. If so, she is bulkier than the Laurenziana Laure.

There was a hushed stillness about the bust of Laura as though I had chanced upon it at the very moment it was about to breathe. Suddenly I was overcome by a desire to kiss the nape of her neck and would surely have done so had it not been for the glass encasing her. *Everything spoke so vividly to my soul.* I began to weep and tremble, my knees about to give way, and I should think there was also the palpitation of the heart that is so much a feature of case histories. And just in case I am thought overly impressionable, I am not thus inclined and would prefer not to make a spectacle of myself in the public arena although I'm not as worried about this as I am about writing breathless prose. Only later, when I thought about it, did I remember, although I'm still not sure there is such a thing, Stendhal syndrome.

*

Visiting the places where famous people lived is more often than not a futile exercise in 'making contact' with their spirits via phantom furniture. The Mozarthaus at Domgasse 5 is in some respects a slightly desperate affair, there being not even a stick of the original furnishings and very little by way of the old décor, the stuccoed ceiling maybe. As for which rooms served as what, this too is all conjecture and, if one were feeling irritable, the entry fee could be seen as a bit of a scam. The alternative take is that it's a rather splendid place, sensitively curated, and a good example of *bel étage* architecture. Several things made my visit valuable. For the two and a half years Mozart lived here, between September 1784 and April 1787, which, depending on one's view, is either no time at all or an enormous slice of his creative life, he composed *Le Nozze di Figaro*, three of the 'Haydn' string quartets and many other works. As well as it being a time of immense productivity it was also, dare one say, one of personal happiness.

We know Mozart had a billiards table and although we can't be sure where it was positioned, because there is no proof of anything, it is not unreasonable to suppose it was kept in the main parlour. The amount he spent on it, 300 florins, was exactly one third of what he paid for his pianoforte, a hefty sum given that the annual rent for the place, the most luxurious of Mozart's several residences, was 460 florins. Mozart was not a man to be deprived of fun. Indeed, it may be the most serious aspect of his music. Thus isolated, fun is profound, mysterious even. We are told Mozart played billiards with his wife Constanze. Sometimes what transports one is the smaller thing against which the bigger is of scant importance. A small key opens the world. Behind the ghostly strains of whichever quartet was playing on the audio guide I heard the *clack click clack* of billiard balls, or is this something I added later? This image of them at play brought the place alive.

You look out the window of that spacious room and straight ahead is the slightly curving street called Blutgasse, which remains absolutely unchanged. You see it through Mozart's eyes. Suppose it is 15 January 1785 and you're outside, you have just turned on to Blutgasse, which leads on to Domgasse, you hear the playing of instruments from an upstairs window, and as you come closer you realise it is a string quartet and you think, *so lovely the sound of music coming from people's houses*, and you walk on, the sound becoming ever fainter. What you do not realise is that in the parlour room upstairs Haydn is sitting in a chair, maybe beside the billiards table, listening to the performance specially put on for him by the much younger Mozart, one of the cycle of six string quartets which the latter dedicated to him. After hearing three on the above date and the rest on 12 February, Haydn said to Mozart's father, 'Before God, and as an honest man, I tell you that your son is the greatest composer known to me either in person or by name'. Such was the generosity of the man who at that point was the most celebrated composer in Europe. So rare, this spirit of deference, you struggle for other instances.

The other thing I heard on the audio guide was a story completely new to me, Mozart's friendly relationship with an African ex-slave called Angelo Soliman. I am surprised this should have escaped the encyclopedic mind of the French writer, Mathias Énard, whose masterpiece *Compass* is set in Vienna. Its main character, Franz Ritter, is a musicologist confined to bed for reasons not exactly clear, and from there he surveys key moments in his life, many of which, most eerily, have also been key moments in mine. Ritter (and by extension Énard) spent considerable time in Syria. I ghosted him or he ghosted me through the streets of Aleppo and Damascus. We ate in the same places and on a couple of occasions encountered the same people, one of them the French Sufi musician, Julien Jâlal Eddine Weiss, whose apartment, now destroyed, was in the Aleppo souk. Énard includes so many actual events and people in his work that it becomes difficult to separate truth from fiction. This surely is his aim, to set alight the borderline between the two. As well as looking back on his own life, Ritter goes back through history and explores the meeting points between classical music and Orientalism. Soliman's absence from Énard's book may be due to Nigeria being not quite east of Vienna, but such was the thinking in Mozart's time that someone from Africa might be considered an Oriental or Turk. It is quite possible that Soliman was the model for the sympathetic figure of Bassa Selim in Mozart's opera *Die Entführung aus dem Serail* ('The Abduction from the Seraglio'). The opera is not for the more faint-hearted of Edward Said's acolytes, who find fault with any who cross a certain longitude, but at the time of its composition, 1781–82, it was a flattering and not wholly inaccurate portrait of Ottoman society. Maybe its plot is a bit on the wild side, but not nearly as improbable as the story of Soliman's life.

Soliman, whose tribal name was Mmadi Make, was of princely origin. As a boy he was taken captive in Nigeria and sold as a slave in Marseilles and from there taken to Sicily where he entered the household of a sympathetic marchioness who oversaw his education. Mmadi's affection for a servant girl called Angelina inspired him to change his name to Angelo. As yet he was not his own man and in 1734 he was gifted to the imperial governor of Sicily, Prince Georg Christian, Prince von Lobkowitz, became his valet and travelling companion, and even joined him on military campaigns, at one point saving his master's life. After the prince's death, Soliman entered the Vienna household of Joseph Wenzel I, Prince of Liechtenstein, where he was made tutor to the prince's heir, Aloys I. It was during this period Soliman married a young widow, the sister of one of Napoleon's generals, which, maybe because of the interracial aspect of the marriage, greatly displeased the prince. Nonetheless, Soliman's rise in Viennese cultural circles was rapid and extended even as far as the Emperor Joseph II. In 1783 he joined the Masonic lodge *Zur Wahren Eintracht* ('To True Harmony') whose membership included many of the cultural luminaries of the period, including Joseph Haydn, the Hungarian poet Ferenc Kazinczy and Wolfgang Amadeus Mozart. There, as 'Angelus Solimanus', he became Grand Master of the lodge.

There is nothing to prove the depth of their friendship, not a single mention of Soliman in Mozart's voluminous correspondence, but what we discover in the Masonic lodge's records is that the two often signed in together, which suggests that they'd met beforehand. If the character of Bassa Selim really was inspired by Soliman, then we may feel free to assume there was at the very least cordiality between them. There is so little solid evidence that its dearth is a boon for the imagination. Soliman, renowned for his high intellect and the fact he could speak several languages, died in 1796 of a stroke, and there begins the terrible story of his posthumous existence, which was enough to make of his previous life a pitiful charade. At the instigation of the emperor – one might well ask how deep their relationship went – and despite the desperate entreaties of Soliman's daughter, Josefine, his corpse was skinned and stuffed and then placed in a cabinet of curiosities at the Imperial Natural History Collection. Decked out with ostrich feathers and beads, Soliman was the perfect illustration of the African savage. He was only granted release from this second enslavement when during the October Revolution of 1848 the part of the museum where he was put on display was set on fire.

Was Soliman no more than an exotic ornament for the Viennese upper classes? And might he himself not have colluded a little? Clearly, he enjoyed his rise to polite society and becoming Grand Master of the Masonic lodge was no mean feat. Mozart was already in his grave when Soliman died and so we can only guess at what his reaction to his friend's fate would have been, but I think it is fair to say he would have been horrified. There has rarely been a great artist in whom one may locate a deeper sense of justice. It informs virtually all his operas, at the end of each there is always a resolution, something which directors today would do well to recognise. Mozart may have been a smutty brat at times, a gambler and a profligate, but there was an abundance of truth, beauty and loyalty in his nature.

When I began to pull together these memories of Vienna I was in the process of going through my mother's effects, two boxes I had shipped over from Canada, which contained books, photographs, old passports and such letters as she had allowed to survive. Included was a copy of *The Illustrated London News*, for the week ending Saturday 21 June 1845. Why it was there, I can't say. I skimmed through the pages to see if there was anything that might relate to family history. There wasn't. Almost immediately, though, my eye fell on a small notice in the section titled 'Epitome of News – Foreign and Domestic'.

> Os-keoau-mai, the wife of Little Wolf, one of the Ioway Indians, died last week in Paris, of an affection of the lungs, brought on by grief for the death of her young child in London. Her husband was unremitting in his endeavours to console her and restore her to the love of life, but she constantly replied – 'No! no! My four children recall me. I see them by the side of the Great Spirit. They stretch out their arms to me, and are astonished that I do not join them.'

This spoke directly to the sense of displacement that marked Angelo Soliman's strange and not wholly unhappy life. Why was the Ioway woman in Paris, so far away from home? My researches led me from her to the American painter George Catlin, who probably was neither wholly bad nor wholly good, his flaws barely distinguishable from his virtues. Catlin brought to Europe several members of the Ioway tribe, whose purpose was to bring his paintings of them to life. It was what in modern parlance we'd call a sales pitch. The Ioway chiefs for their part were curious to see of what exactly their white settlers were made. They, however, were the ones on display. Charles Baudelaire, who attended the exhibition, remarks on 'the proud, free character and the noble expression of these splendid fellows', although in calling them savages he fails to rise above the tenor of the times. We can't really judge him from our self-righteous perspective. The printed notice in the *Illustrated London News* was a tiny window into an immense tragedy. When I copied it out for a friend of mine, he immediately replied, saying it would be a perfect starting point for an opera. He was not being facetious. Maybe my mother was sending me a message. Although she was a difficult woman, when it came to the oppressed of this world she was sympathetic to the point of disliking all else.

The next snippet of news following that of Os-keoau-mai's death is rather more mundane, but what caught my eye was, although hardly worthy of note, its geographical location:

> The Austrian papers announce that a merchant of Venice has obtained permission to construct a railway from Verona to Bregenz, by way of Roerede, Tirent, Bolzin, Meran, Landeck, and Feldkirch, to effect a close communication between the Austrian seaports. The plan is said to have been very favourably received at Vienna.

Vienna is not a place I'd choose to live. Firstly, there is the food, the ubiquitous Wiener schnitzel, a clumsy relative of the Italian *cotoletta alla milanese*. Apparently, Austrians enjoy it enough to make an evening of it at a restaurant, when they can have it just as easily at home, more cheaply too. All you need is a frying pan and a sufficient lack of finesse. And then my friend Eric Ormsby singles out for special praise the *Tafelspitz*, what many of us would call boiled meat, but then what's to be said of a man for whom the hot dog is the epitome of high cuisine? The pastries, though, are divine. Secondly, the coffee, though excellent, is expensive. Thirdly, when one turns the corner of any street, one finds exactly what one expects to see, the city's architectural regularity being one of the things for which it is accorded praise. I abhor the straight line. These things aside, and, after all, nobody is inviting me to live there, I'm glad I went so that I might bury the hatchet I'd kept sharp for four decades. Surely a city that brought out the best in Mozart, Haydn, Schubert, Beethoven and Mahler ought to bring out the better in me. Most vitally, I had been forced back upon myself into a deeper consideration of the soul or whatever it was that Vienna drew out of me. I wonder if what we call soul is not in fact a conduit to the interconnectedness between all things whereby it might be possible, after quitting our shells, to take up residence inside a bird's song.

String theory is, poetically, the most satisfying of all theories, even or maybe *especially* to those who don't understand it. The idea that all forces in the universe, even those that would appear unrelated, are part of a single framework is perhaps the closest we can come to any understanding of what we call God, or, in keeping with ancient pagan thinkers – for what is a pagan but a Christian parboiled – a synthesis of all nature's forces. *I seek a connection between all this: these are distances the stammering mind cannot hold.*

I have not yet unpicked all the tangles in Hersch's weighty opus, nor am I ever likely to. I don't know whether the marble bust really is Petrarch's Laura, nor, again, am I ever likely to, and what it would be to know of what Mozart and Angelo Soliman spake, but if, as certain physicists argue, there'll come a point when time goes backwards, the wait will be a long one. What was it about Vienna and its willowy muse that I should have been rewarded not once, not twice, but thrice?

From *gridlines*

JANE DURAN

after Agnes Martin

'The Peach' 1964

graphite and ink on paper
mounted on board

well, it's forgotten now
that peach I knew

I bit into
that gave me back

only beige, graphite,
ink, sanity

and orchard after orchard

'The Tree' 1964

oil paint and graphite on
canvas

I must visit my tree
one last time

so I will have no regrets

before it disperses entirely
before it disappears

into the wind
of grey rectangles

grid

some days I also search
for its certainty

with tape or string
a T-square, pencil

or paint. I lean into it

here and there a tremor
in my hand indicates

a slight give, a looseness
or elasticity

the scouring

how will it end

the way the wind
loosens things

scours, scores
and abandons?

After the electroshock
therapy at Bellevue

and she takes off
in a white pickup truck

old landmarks
vanish

her eyes squinting
in the sunlight

her downcast eyes
her bewildered eyes

road trip 1967–68

'The solitary life is full of
terrors...'
– Agnes Martin

ah the dust I kick up
disturbing the landscape

when I turn my pickup
in a blur of desert

Here is country I recognise
a rejection, flatland

and the innocent
pastimes of air

whenever I stop
and roll down

my window
key in the ignition

spoon in a tin cup

For Anne Stevenson (1933–2020)

PETER SCUPHAM

Lament for a Maker

Dear Anne, our shooting star, you've left us all
'your lovelies weeping on a faraway shore':
husbands, friends, loves, admirers – a host
who suffered your hilarious devastations
tense with quaking joy. I see your hands
compassionately poised above my birthday cake,
the steel plied deftly. Though it winced
the blood was swiftly staunched, and we were left
with crumbs of sharp, sustaining comfort.

Oh, attic nights, when salt could lose no savour
rubbed in the wounds your rapier-talk inflicted.
As hours grew smaller, your imprecations
and efficacious 'fucks' rose up the chimney
to make Orion blush, or Father Christmas,
as poets known, unknown, yet to be born,
crept skinned and howling into dusty corners,
bobbed and hovered in the whisky fumes,
drowned in tides of laughter, fulmination.

Tutoring found you in a sprawl of drafts,
a chatter of poems flattering themselves,
loved to distraction by fond parenting,
while you, the musical philosopher,
rational magician, saw clean through them
as they read each other in woeful admiration.
Nagaina, cobra, how you fixed your prey
with unrelenting eyes, until that moment
when fear and folly turned to fun and feasting.

And now it seems that you have packed your bag
for one more residency in that country
you never could believe in, where Mr Darwin
at work on the fossil records of the angels
considers the embryonic state of wings,
watched by an affable chowder of young cats.
I glimpsed you as you hitched a passing broomstick,
your elfin face stern, yet benevolent.
Even white witches have to ride on something.

In Conversation with John Ash

JEFFREY KHARS

This interview is taken from a series of conversations I had with John Ash in the spring of 2010. We met several times and always chatted around four or five in the afternoon for an hour to an hour and a half, when the sunlight would come through his windows for a short while. This was the best time to catch him because he usually read and wrote in the early afternoon, sipping on his rakı, so by the time we spoke later he was lubricated but still cogent, which often meant he was feeling contrary. Interviewing John took patience. He hated to be photographed, refused to sell his manuscripts – even though he certainly could have used the money – and rarely acquiesced to even the shortest of interviews. I persevered because I knew his health was more fragile than he was willing to admit and he was both an important writer and a friend.

Jeffrey: You said your father was a geography teacher. Is that how you became a traveller?

John: I think possibly because, before my father got married and settled down and had children, he would go all over Europe. He had friends in Vienna, so he'd go all the way across Europe on his motorbike.

When did you write your first poem?

I can tell you very precisely. I was reading a book by Brigid Brophy. She mentioned that the great Watteau painting *The Departure for Cythera* was actually the *Departure from Cythera*. I thought, 'Okay, that's interesting.' She provided very strong evidence that this title is completely wrong because there's a shrine to Venus in the painting, so it's actually a very melancholy painting. I just thought it was very interesting, so I wrote a poem called *Departure from Cythera* which has never been published and probably should not be.

How old were you?

I was still in my teens.

Who was a great influence on you when you were young?

When I started out trying to be a poet, Roy Fisher was the only guy I had. I mean he was the only person whose work was obviously influenced by American and European poetry. I actually corresponded with him as well though I never met him. The standard thing was you had to write something that sounded a bit like Philip Larkin. Philip Larkin is a wonderful poet, but that was not what I wanted to write. I was reading American and French poetry.

Who were the French poets?

Laforgue of course. Mallarmé, Apollinaire. But they are of course now considered totally old hat in France. And René Char. He provided the text for Pierre Boulez's wonderful *Le Soleil des eaux*.

How did you become so involved with music?

It was from my father. My father was a big classical-music buff, particularly Mozart and Mahler, and he was something of a pioneer, because in the fifties and sixties, until people like Leonard Bernstein took up Mahler, he was regarded as vulgar and bombastic. Then I got more into twentieth-century music.

How did you choose to live in Istanbul?

I wanted to get out of New York, and I had already been to Istanbul several times. I felt it would be one of the few places that wouldn't be an anticlimax after New York. It's just as crazy as New York

Was it hard to make the adjustment to living here?

Not really. I was very lucky because I quickly acquired a patron, Selçuk Altun.

You live in Galata on the European side. What is it that attracted you to the place?

Apartments were going for a song. The area has now become very high end.

Why stay here then?

Well, it's familiar as home should be and my neighbourhood is filled with wonderful cats.

Do you ever miss England?

I do sort of miss my favourite part of England, which is Herefordshire. It's a landscape with very slow rivers. It is very peaceful and has lots of medieval abbeys and tame birds living in the abbeys. They'll actually perch on your hand. But I couldn't live there because there's nothing around there... apart from the cat from the neighbouring farmhouse, which would come in through the skylight and curl up with me.

What poets are you reading these days?

I read the poets I love like Cavafy, Turkish poets like Oktay Rıfat, and Andrew Marvell. 'The Garden' is one of the greatest poems in English. Right now I'm reading the fabulous Armenian poet Krikor Naregatsi.

Who do you enjoy that's more formal?

Pope is funny. One of my favourite poems is Pope's epistle to Lord Burlington. It's giving him advice about building his new mansion, so it's all about architecture. It's wonderful. I didn't initially like Alexander Pope at all. I can't stand 'The Rape of the Lock'. I'm not a great admirer of the heroic couplet, but then I discovered this poem and it sort of changed my opinion. It's not just humour in the epistle to Lord Burlington. It is – though it's in heroic couplets – a great essay on architecture. Apart from Pope, the eighteenth century wasn't dripping with great poets. It was a century of great prose. Who else did you mention?

Byron.

Byron is the greatest comic poet in English. I mean, just his rhymes are hysterically funny. He's so awful. I can never remember this couplet accurately. It says something like: 'If you think 'twas philosophy this did, I can't help thinking puberty assisted'. I think that's it.

The other thing about Byron is he was really an eighteenth-century poet.

Oh, he was. All his good poetry is wildly anti-romantic. There is nothing romantic about Byron.

I can see why Kenneth Koch and the New York poets looked to Byron as a figure of such importance because they loved writing as a pleasure.

That's the great thing about the New York poets. They actually enjoyed writing poetry. It was not an academic exercise.

You brought Kenneth Koch to Istanbul. How did that come about?

It was actually at the invitation of Yapı Kredi, a local bank here that sponsors a great many cultural events and has its own press. Of course, Ashbery came as well. I just helped arrange affairs.

When did John come here?

It must have been shortly after I moved here, I suppose. I think he was in Greece or somewhere nearby, so I said, 'Why don't you come here and give a reading?' And so he did.

What's your favourite story about Ashbery and Koch? If I recall it was about them arguing and bickering with each other...

Well, that's what they did. And then the next day they both rang me up and complained about the other one. I said: 'Well, I had a very nice time. What's your problem?' I just didn't understand what was going on. They had this long rivalry I knew nothing about and was not interested in.

Do you have any favourite poems by Koch or Ashbery that you go back to again and again?

My favourite Kenneth Koch poem is 'The Problem of Anxiety'. Kenneth had this wonderful way of addressing real problems that everybody has in their lives in this completely batty way. The first poem by Ashbery that really wowed me was 'As One Put Drunk into the PacketBoat'. The title is also a quotation from Andrew Marvell.

People are always saying Ashbery is a big influence on you.

Well... I owe a great debt to John Ashbery. Though I haven't seen him in several years, he's a close friend and a wonderful person. He's the person who invited me to New York and sort of looked after me. He was great.

When I read The Anatolikon, To the City, *or* The Parthian Stations, *I don't necessarily think of your style and Ashbery's as being so similar.*

Well, *Branching Stairs* has nothing to do with Ashbery at all. The difference is, I write about history.

Another writer you've told some really great stories about is Harry Mathews.

Harry as far as I know is still doing fine in Paris. You don't know what to believe and he's not going to give you any hints. So, either he *was* working for the CIA – which everybody thought and which he then furiously denied so he thought, 'Right, well, I'll write a novel saying I was working for the CIA.' It's a very funny book. I think Harry is a really underestimated writer. His big books are the amazingly named *The Sinking of the Odradek Stadium* and *Tlooth*. The syllable 'Tlooth' is uttered by a prophetic bog near Venice. His novels are fabulous. I think they are among the greatest of the twentieth century.

This love of twentieth-century classical music is something you share with the New York School.

Well, they are all very devoted to it. Harry studied under Nadia Boulanger to become a conductor.

Favourite poems of Frank O'Hara?

'In Memory of My Feelings', 'Memoir of Sergei O', and of course, 'Lana Turner Has Collapsed'.

Let's not forget Ronald Firbank.

I have his complete works. Firbank was a great stylist. He's obviously very funny, but that's not the really important thing. He bent English into this completely personal style, which is really weird and beautiful. And also he had a wonderful ear. He had a character called Lady Parvula de Panzoust.

I know you love Freya Stark's writing.

She's my hero.

How about Gertrude Bell and T. E. Lawrence?

He has a wildly over-ornate style from the bits I've read. I prefer my girls Freya and Gertrude.

We haven't spoken about Gertrude Bell.

She's a very fine prose writer. She doesn't over-elaborate and she can be extremely, almost brutally direct on occasion. What really drew me to her was her account of the so-called Dead Cities in northern Syria, and that's what made me want to go there.

What did you learn from Dame Freya in your travel writing?

I like the way she combines so many different genres; autobiography, memoir, travel writing, history, like her magnificent description of the Battle of Magnesia. *Rome on the Euphrates* is a masterpiece.

The Tang Chinese poets were also quite important to you.

There's actually one particular volume translated by A. C. Graham I love. I think they're wonderful translations but I've never been able to find anything else that he translated. Weird. It's still in print in Penguin and I always have it with me. It contains poems by Li Ho, Li Shang Yin. Li Shang Ying I'm particular fond of. He wrote a great poem called 'Peonies'. The notes to the translation are much longer than the poem because every line is absolutely compacted with meaning and allusions. And there's Tu Fu as well. Li Po doesn't really count.

This is an essential book? You take it with you everywhere?

Yeah.

Why don't you come here and read it?

Here's 'Peonies' by Li Shang Yin:
The brocade curtains have just rolled back. Behold the Queen of Wei.
Still he piles up the embroidered quilts, Prince O in Yüeh.
Drooping hands disturb, tip over, pendants of carved jade:
Snapping waists compete in the dance, fluttering saffron skirts.
Shi Ch'ung's candles – but who would clip them?
The Hsün Yu's brazier, where no incense fumes.
I who was given in a dream the brush of many colours
Wish to write on petals a message to the clouds of morning.

Didn't you work on some translation from Chinese at one point?

They're published in one of my collections. My boyfriend at the time, Tsung Woo and I, got heavily into translating Tang poetry. 'The Grave of Little Su', that's a good one. Ah, 'Don't Go Out the Door':
Heaven is inscrutable,
Earth keeps its secrets:
The nine-headed monster eats our souls.

Essential books?

Poems of the Late T'ang by A. C. Graham, collected works of Cavafy, collected works of George Trakl, Ashbery's *Houseboat Days*. There are several books by Ashbery, but that's my particular favourite. Oh, Seferis. The best translations are by a guy called Rex Warner. I haven't mentioned Ingeborg Bachmann.

What makes a good translation?

A bad translation just doesn't ring true. The tone of voice is wrong. Actually, one of my favourite poems by Ingeborg Bachmann is 'Great Landscape Near Vienna'. It's wonderful but virtually untranslatable.

Like Paul Celan?

Paul Celan *is* completely untranslatable. The number of people who can claim to understand Celan I would think is minute. I mean he really is hermetic. Some of his early
stuff is relatively easy, and I think he's a great poet, but the later stuff becomes so hermetic.

The abstract expressionist painters could be seen as quite hermetic. What do you think of someone like Willem de Kooning?

I never really got Willem de Kooning until they had this big show – presumably at the MOMA – and I was knocked out by it. I just thought it was wonderful. Even some of the late stuff. Well, he had Alzheimer's, but just before he really lost it, he produced some beautiful stuff. And then because of my interest in de Kooning, I discovered Elaine de Kooning, who I like even more than her husband. She's a magnificent painter.

The women were overshadowed in that period.

Very much. The men were terrible, terrible sexists. Elaine was absolutely magnificent and she painted on a really big, heroic scale, but only became known after he died.

Would you say Elaine is one of your essential painters?

I'm very interested in all the Abstract Expressionists. I like a lot of Pollock's work. *Autumn Rhythm* is superb. The paintings have great physical presence that reproductions can't convey.

Like Rothko...

Again, Rothko reproductions are no use at all. You have to stand in front of the painting for quite a long time. And Arshile Gorky of course, who more or less started Abstract Expressionism.

Let's talk about essential music.

Well, Mahler is definitely one, the entire Second Viennese School, which is Schoenberg, Berg, Webern and Zemlinsky, who until recently tended to get overlooked, and he's one of the great twentieth-century composers, certainly one of the greatest songwriters of the twentieth century. Kurt Weill, completely essential, and Ferruccio Busoni and Dallapiccola. *Ulysses*, his enormous opera, is very beautiful, particularly Ulysses's farewell.

Essential composers... Debussy. Particularly the piano music. The *Etudes*, amazing, just inexhaustible. You can listen to them over and over again. The *Préludes* are pretty good too. And of course he was also a great orchestrator.

Do you like Stockhausen?

I think he's a piece of shit. There was an interesting piece by him called *Trans*. It has two orchestras beating the shit out of each other over a half an hour. I don't think he's a very musical composer. Well, I mean the thing with music at that time was IRCAM, Pierre Boulez's underground musical bunker. They produced fuckin' awful music. There is no other way of putting it. I mean, this stuff was unlistenable, of no interest to anyone else apart from the people producing it, which is of course what turned a lot of people off to twentieth-century (classical) music. It didn't give any kind of the things they expected of music.

Stravinsky is probably my favourite composer of all time. The concision and wit of Stravinsky were very important to me. I think he was one of the great minds of the twentieth century. He never wrote a crap piece of music. He was extremely witty... and so was his wife, Vera! There's a great moment, I think it was in Santiago, Chile, and he was asked this rather obscure question about his collaboration with a Swiss dramatist during the First World War. He said, 'I don't remember. We were drunk most of the time.' And there was this shocked silence, into which Stravinsky breaks with: 'I have always been a drunkard. I would rather be a drunkard than a prisoner of my neighbour's opinion.'

Poems

Yeow Kai Chai

Shadow Cabinet

an anagrammatic subtext

tapping the top rail
he gives you a death stare
left hand gripping
the arm support
the right holding
a dodgy dossier
sexed up
with saddam's spies
secret weapons
bubbly green gas
in glass containers
such delicate bombs
of fear contagion

a threat piping plot
thy hosts add eerie guava
ping dreg than fling
to pat hem purrs
hide light throng
rosy dogs died
dupes ex
dadaists phew isms
ancestors weep
leggy babes burn
a nonsensical grist
a cobbled ethics sum
a faction forgone

Shadow Cabinet II

'It sounds sad, but it felt like I'd lost someone. A friend.'
– Kate Robinson, an Amy Winehouse lookalike, after the death of the singer

walking out the mirror
you don't quite know
who are left behind
reflection having merged
with the object
larger than life
in the eye of posterity
a ventriloquist's echo
a mimic's day-glo
radiant as memory
still as a slough
one smells a rat
scourge unchurched
mine untwined
from this gizmo
whirring nearer...

a mightier rot now lurk
unquiet wok toy nod
behead hinter wolf
drag fleece hot virgin men
bewitch the jot
feral earthling
etherise yo nifty poet
a voiceless thorn quit
magma icy idols
dreamy animator
assail lug sloth
arsenals motel
coerced hunch gurus
tedium new inn
fights zoom rim
rawer in her ring...

Channel Surfers: Eight Unrelated Scenes

The angry mob is coming after the fugitive, armed with tommy guns and Maasai spears...

The Fugees, decked out in Tommy Hilfiger, chew Wrigley's Spearmint, impervious to the tide of the audience rushing up...

Adrift in the open sea, Tom Jones aims a speargun at a school of marlin while one slippery eel leaps out of the skullduggery...

The orphan spots a tommyknocker posing with a skull as a spearhead before the latter disappears into the funfair crowd...

Beware: spear phishers are targeting Tommy Lee Jones fans with the promise to leak the winner of Survivor in an e-mail scam involving diehard fans...

Thomas the Tank Engine is on the run with Dr Richard Kimble; both pursued by bounty hunters all dressed up as spearfishing enthusiasts...

The louder the runaway bride screams, the hungrier the zombies become, is the Spearmint's rank correlation, reckons watchmaker Thomas Earnshaw who adjusts the alarm accordingly...

Confronting the bullies at the orphanage, Spearow shields poor Tommy Boy in the scullery as the Artful Dodger slips out into an alley...

No Rabbit

Rebecca Perry

I once wrote a poem which appeared to mourn the death of a pet.

After reading it, a friend asked about the pet, which he presumed to be a dog.

I told him that the dog was a figment of my imagination, as was its death and the scenario in which I imagined its memorial:

the person I was with in the poem, the cold evening and the frost that formed on the grass.

The friend, a poet, seemed annoyed and disappointed.

He had wanted to be in on the trick

even if he couldn't be sure what would be pulled from the hat.

Lying comes with many responsibilities, or as many as we choose to acknowledge, or none.

Or it needn't be called lying at all.

The two scenes I described in the poem were not retellings but I have,
in other streams of time, known the deaths of animals and humans,

and dark nights and frost on the grass,

and being in the quiet company of another person in the aftermath of grief, as has practically everyone else.

The poem, in part, had been about how we manage death in ritual or through contact with the living, or how we fail to manage it at all.

The poem had also mentioned a person I love, though not in the context of my love for them.

I suppose this had been for my benefit alone: a private word with myself.

Perhaps that was the real travesty of the poem.

I have an absurd sense that love poems without pain in them are shameless, and that anecdotal honesty is as much a figment of the imagination as hallucinating rain through a dusty window.

Years after I wrote about the fictional dog, I sat on the shore of a beach very far from home, surrounded by small, translucent crabs popping out of their holes

as that same person, the one I loved, walked with their back to me, through the waves, to swim in a rough sea.

In those moments, the sun was setting brilliant silver on the surface of the water.

I was thinking then that I was afraid of so much and them so little.
Months passed and this was shown to be false.

More time went by. The friend died, the poet, and along with it his side of the story, the knots in the grain.

Memory continues to mix sediment into the water. Familiar smells disturb the air.

Light glows in from the hallway.

If you fail to close the door on a poem, how can it sleep? Anyone could look in.

Play It All the Way Through, First – but Slowly

KIRSTY GUNN

At five years old I was sent to piano lessons at seven thirty on a Friday morning with a teacher who wore pretty, glittery nail polish but was otherwise terrifying. Seven thirty on a dark winter's morning in Wellington is not what anyone imagines when they think about New Zealand, and those mornings were dark and they were wintry and the piano teacher was not at all happy to be up in them, teaching scales and arpeggios to a child who could not seem to get to the end of a run of notes without making a mistake, or having to pause, or start again. 'No! No! No!' she would cry out, rapping me over the knuckles with a heavy wooden ruler she kept close by for such occasion – the glittery polish on the hand that did the rapping not so pretty then. 'For goodness' sake, can't you reach the end of at least something without stopping?'

That phrase has been with me over these past few months as I've been going without pause at the works of Henry James. For in the past, reading James, how I did stop. There would be this sentence with its wildly, awkwardly Jamesian punctuation here, another paragraph, stiff with his subordinate clauses, there. Where's the subject? I would fret. To what object does that adjective pertain? There were the endless reams of double negatives to be played over in the mind and sorted, words to be held up at and gone over for additional nuance – so not simple opinions, but animadversions; canicular for dog days, impeachment for request, and so on, along with countless asseverations and the affixing of prefixes to so many perfectly good verbs. As notes with accidentals poked into the bars may challenge any kind of sight reading, so did this prose affix difficulties upon the eye of the young reader. And the list went on. Studying James had always densely seemed to be a lesson in grammar and parse-ing as much as it was his vision of the world and its lovely things and who might get them, as generally seemed to be case in the novels I read then, those spoils of Poynton and all the rest of it. Was there anything going on in these stories apart from the wanting and having? Was there anything in there for me?

But this year, ever since the first lockdown, I decided I might just return to the writer other writers call 'The Master'. I wanted to see if I could uncover something of a conversation I'd started a few years ago, about the surfaces of writing in fiction, the way a novel might attempt something of the poem's neat alignment of perception and expression; I wanted to invigorate the memory of that earlier discussion with a sort of seminar series for one, is how I've put it to myself. I began with *The Art of the Novel* and have been marching right on through with a reading and rereading programme of the novels, sticking Post-it notes into paragraphs and phrases that in the past might have held me up with some prevision of further complexities and alterations of plot but that now give me nothing but delight, all the way through to the very end.

For how James is changed to me now! At the end of the year, and with most of the shelf in view – the Penguin Modern Classics series, mostly, but some nice older editions there too – I think I'm beginning to understand why I've always needed to know more about these books. For the set here before me, I see now is not actually a set of novels at all – in the sense of that tiresome concept of a fixed content and approach, one book pretty much like another – which would be too boring for words. What I have here instead, I think, is rather more of an adventure in fiction, a test, a series of excitements and risks... A project, with none of the novel series' tendency to ease into repeated facility. Instead, I have at my disposal a run of quite separate narratives that are not so much stories as constructions, ornate complications of syntax and phrasing with varying counterpoint of vocabulary set alongside the rhythm of a language which James is developing for himself, anew, remaking with every title. So it's not so much the great piles of wealth and who might wrangle their way into grabbing it that's at stake here, on endless repeat; nor is the point the pricking and poking by various older women in order to achieve marriage for some young sprite. Nor are they even about failed loves, this run of *The Portrait of a Lady* and *The Bostonians* and *Roderick Hudson*, or broken loves, *The Awkward Age*, *The Golden Bowl*, or loves that should never have got started up in the first place, *The Europeans*, *The Wings of the Dove*, as is the way with so many so-called 'period' novels amongst which many may claim James seems to play his part. Nor are they about, in the end – though they certainly include – the lovely houses and the things inside them, their balustraded gardens and New England fanlights set in scenery that might be painted it's so lovely... No. These novels are not as much about their subjects as I once thought. It's the telling of them, that everyone talks about, and writes about, of course, that's at issue here. 'Ah, those sentences', a Modernist scholar murmured to me when I told her what I was up to; and there's Woolf alongside, wishing if only James 'were content to say less and suggest more'. But to my mind, there's no use coming up against the sentences as a block. For the same sentences, surely, are the very gist. These novels must tell. And tell, and tell. Their whole being is in it. And it's the telling, the complications and the sheer fun of doing that in all kinds of different ways – polishing up some anecdote or other James picked up at a bright luncheon or party, giving it a twist and altering its fixings so that it might whirl and shine like a gilded top – that makes it new. Not a thing about a thing at all, this fiction of The Master, but a thing all by itself.

For these years past, then, when I've been somewhat snobbish myself about novels I deemed as being rather snobbish, taking them, as I did back then, at face value and held up at every turn by various individuals who on the whole were either avaricious or in some other way wanting, were just unpleasant or shallow or pompous or too taken up with only their own thoughts, I was failing to see that James's characters are, rather, those who might be for him, as Aristotle would have had it, 'stage figures' – people made out of the stuff of art, set in the praxis of event and counter event. They are no more straining to be 'real' than Clytemnestra is, or Oedipus – even to the most ardent Freudian – may want to be. It's how they're thought about, drawn and presented that's the thing. And those women of his, those terrifying, wonderful, shocking, wry, brilliant or stupid central characters who express prime agency in most of the stories were, I think, never intended to be a Dorothea or Becky Sharpe or a Natasha. They are portraits of various kinds of ladies, not the sitters themselves.

There's variation here, in what I'm getting at, because of course Isabel Archer is a delight of a young woman, and a terrific model of youth's idealism and verve for young (especially), though older readers, too, to meet. But she arrives on the page very much drawn up and painted in by her narrator; for it is that person who has figured her with a set of thoughts and values all cast in the smiling tones of his loving condescension. Altogether, it's his light – that stage light James loves to write about in his introductions to the novels – cast upon the people in his stories which brings them to our attention; it's not natural. It's not supposed to be. So here I am, slow to the game, no doubt, coming to the end of my seminar series, and the truth is out. Henry James's novels aren't about the moral trajectory of a bildunsroman or romance or intrigue of the realist novel doing its realist thing – a mimesis performed, albeit, with a Master's infinite tact and sense of gentility. These characters of his, these stories – based as they are on the stuff of gossip – are simply made up, beautifully and fully, of words. Not only 'those sentences', then, but words, infinite and individual, played out in myriad combinations. So yes, Fleda Vetch, Rowland Mallet and Madame Merle, and all the rest speak the way they do – oh, how they speak! – and their personalities and histories and sensibilities are dressed almost entirely of those speeches, along with their glorious, informant names. But the speeches and description of and around them is studded and starred with literary affect and the accessory of a most self-conscious vocabulary; the whole body of the tale covered over in the rich mantle of presentation James himself, arch playwright as he always wanted to be, loves to give it. Here comes a paragraph entire, from *The Europeans*, one sister remarking upon another, which shows precisely just where this kind of wordsmithsmanship might take one: 'Charlotte gazed at her sister again. Gertrude's imagination seemed to her to be running riot. She had always known that Gertrude had a great deal of imagination – she had been very proud of it. But at the same time she had always felt that it was a dangerous and irresponsible faculty; and now, to her sense, for the moment, it seemed to threaten to make her sister a strange person who should come in suddenly, as from a journey, talking of the peculiar and possibly unpleasant things she had observed. Charlotte's imagination took no journeys whatever; she kept it, as it were, in her pocket, with the other furniture of this receptacle – a thimble, a little box of peppermint and a morsel of court-plaster.' You see? Those pocket items? How they move characters from being people into strange and stravaiging nouns? And all done so neatly, simply by following along, one thing to another – this by way of example, and just one dotted fraction of the outfit complete.

There are exceptions: I think the kind eyes of the Mississippian in *The Bostonians* is one of the most electrifying descriptions of desire that I have ever read, of one person really, really wanting another, and so fully, and attractively, expressed in just half a sentence, even while he's at the same time annihilating the feminist cause and therefore shouldn't be of interest to his interlocutor, a supposed spokeswoman for it – but is. 'Lord, how you're perverted; you, the very genius', he murmurs to Verena Tarrant as he keeps her lingering on a park bench, and she can't leave him, she can't. He's looking at her 'with the kindest eyes'. There is also a moment, in *The Golden Bowl*, of utter sexual deceit laid bare in a nursery chant of their assignation set up by a pair of adulterers that horrifies in its easy acknowledgement of culpability – like a murderer smiling cheerily at his victim while he slits her throat. '"Glo'ster, Glo'ster," as you say, making it sound like an old song... I'm sure Glo'ster, Glo'ster will be charming' sings out the invincible (nearly) Charlotte Stant – as though it means nothing, and in those seconds it's done, what these two are going to do. And there's another revelation, in that same novel, when one of the pair, who has been caught out by his wife, simply absolves himself by not talking. Not talking, in a James novel, is a way of disappearing – and for the deceptive Prince a quick and reliable way out of being cast as a cad. So yes, there are these moments, for sure, and others, of what I think of as pure action, when the deed overrides the description of it. But they are only moments, and on the whole I have come to the pleasurable conclusion that it's the complex surface of narrative, not only the sentences' richly embroidered length, that provides pleasure – for its own sake – in any of these marvellous novels, more than the theatricalities of scene or act in appropriation of fortune or exercise of will.

As far as I can see so far, James doesn't write about this in *The Art Of the Novel*, or include it, as Michael Schmidt quotes in his *The Novel: a biography*, in James's letters and remarks to Howells about the 'paraphernalia' in his work . That was about stuff not syntax, and what side of the Atlantic one wanted to be on. So this is just me, in this essay, having the time of my life realising that these books I used to think were so 'wordy', stumbling over them with cries of 'Get to the point!', are exactly that. That they never necessarily wanted to get to the point. 'I admit I can't be bothered to snuff out his meaning', Woolf may have confessed – but he wasn't necessarily hell-bent on 'meaning'. The words are the books. They are the experience of them, one after another. And like notes in a sonata or scale I have needed to come to understand how they all fit so beautifully together, the accidentals, sharps and flats, in order to learn how to play.

Much has been written of James's interest in theatre, of his failed incursions, and the vast appeal held out for him reaching an audience in literature that might echo and reflect the same applause and glamour of the West End. That he was after that particular sort of fame is well established. This all comes out – with nothing at all, as I say, of my own admixtures contained within it – in his writing about them, the turning of a story into a sort of production. I seem to remember that was part of my undergraduate class in James – but it didn't make reading him into the sort of non-stop whizz of arpeggios that might constitute the rap'less ease and delight of my play of James now. *The Art of the Novel*, altogether, is quite something. Imagine going through all your novels, as they are prepared for republication in beautiful deep-plum bindings, and making decisions about them: whether you like them or not, how this was done, whether you're happy with that. What was in your mind when you sat down to get started? What difficulties were there to be overcome? I decided to read all of *The Art of the Novel*, before I went back to the novels themselves, both those I knew, and those I didn't – and I'm really glad I did. Because there's no doubt that James makes a great deal of all the theatricality – he's at pains to show it. 'The first half of a fiction insists ever on figuring to me as the stage or theatre for the second half', he writes in his introduction to *The Tragic Muse*, that story of acting and actresses, inspiration and thwart. 'Each of my "lamps"', he writes for *The Awkward Age*, 'would be the light of a single "social occasion"... and would bring out to the full the latent colour of the scene.' Adding, 'The beauty of the conception was in this approximation of the respective divisions of my form to the successive Acts of a Play – as to which it was more than ever a case for charmed capitals', and enjoying, as he always does, his own proud entrance to the observation: the writer coming in on the writing. The director, playwright and producer stepping forward on to his own stage. There's a lot of that kind of thing. All of which only makes it of a more concentrated interest to me that I've come away after reading his novels with a greater feel not so much for the Master's as Hamlet's sense of a play. The author, to my mind, protesteth too much in *The Art of the Novel* about this reveal or that, one act after another, when for me the whole experience has been so clearly, simply, well, 'Words, words, words...'. The poetics of Henry James is now a concept that has taken root for me and I see novels growing out of it. I see Woolf's plant in the surrounding earth of this idea, and Mansfield's Aloe. I see Gertrude Stein's rose and much of her fiction, and I see, how I see, beautifully, absolutely everything of Muriel Spark.

But of course the theatre must be there and I must acknowledge it, and be in the spirit of things. James scholarship is so definite about it, as was James himself, about what he intends – and so it's all very well my having these ideas but neither do I read James talking about the make-up of a sentence or the use of italics or repetition or inverted commas or curious words that jump in and alter, as I have so happily focused upon to further my own pleasure. Those 'he made her incongruous offers – ' etc. etc. as I read in *The Spoils of Poynton*, for example, as though I may be reading a poem by Frank O'Hara, 'a travelling-rug, a massive clock, a table for breakfast in bed, and above all, in a resplendent binding, a set of somebody's "works"'... That's my take on this, I own it. None of that sort of appreciation is in his own study. His remarks are richly reserved for that stage management – 'the acute constructional', as he puts it, and the need to obey '"scenic" law' – and it's all there, for sure. The novels themselves are enseamed with theatrical goings-on, ejaculations, doors opening into the unexpected, farcical meetings, stagey set-ups... All massively spotlit and backdropped, each one exquisitely painted – and there's much more to say about this, the painted nature of the surfaces and subjects and backdrops of the stories – whether in the school of European, English or American style. Still, even still... These other ideas of mine, of words as items on the page... They won't go away. They persist. They are inside my reading and there they fizz and ignite: so one word here. Another. The next thing, there's a whole book of them.

I started getting interested in James a few years ago when I was writing a novel of my own which I wanted to make chiefly about syntax and presentation – about the challenges of preventing things happening when all you really want is pages turned by language alone – and it was my colleague and friend, Woolf scholar and poet, the late Jim Stewart, who set me at the path I arrived upon fully in 2020. For there was James in his novels with these beautifully wrought conversations that are his trademark, bearing little relation to the way anyone would actually speak – with critic James Wood and many others making much of this, the way 'he transfers his own acute sensitivity to verbal calibration onto his characters' as Wood puts it – even in the most artfully constructed period piece, let alone those written in his rather more emancipated era. Yet that didn't stop his stories counting as... stories. So, Jim thought, here was a writer who could teach me a thing or two about convention and narration. And we started a conversation then, he and I, about not so much caring for activity and kinetics in a novel as simply loving the sheer sound of it, the cadence and throng and rhythm, and about a someone – and mightily skilled at it he was – who seemed to want to practise exactly that. 'A great writer,' Jim said (I was uncertain then if I thought the same), who had already well effected the kind of novel which might be as intriguing as you like, full of interest on the page, but where the love story or human drama or the happy ending or what have you could just, actually, as I ended up writing myself in my own attempt, *Caroline's Bikini*, 'go hang'.

So yes, I was having these lovely discussions with my dear and learned colleague who was – I see now, looking back and why oh why hadn't I seen, as Maisie does, by the end of that novel, and so knows? – quietly telling me how much use James was going to be to me in this project. We talked a great deal about that set-up of his – the sheer common sense that went into the planning of novelistic situations, and the unpacking of the ideas behind the whole thing in dialogue and the exposition of conversation, as Jim and I had it – showing so much of what was needed by way of plot development in discussion's active back and forth. 'The divine principle of the scenario, Kirsty,' Jim said, 'I'll look that out for you, where James writes about that. I think it may have been in *The Art of Fiction...*', but in fact it turned out to be in a letter James wrote quoted by Leon Edel in his *Henry James: A Life*, which I found included in an email Jim had written to me tucked into a beaten-up copy of *The Ambassadors*. After Jim's death I realised I was confronting a great gap in my life – with that dear man having left the stage – but here also, this year, I've seen coming forward to meet me, as though by way of making up for it (and one never forgets how books altogether help one make up for all kinds of lost and lovely things), two thoroughly instructive James-es – to help out. There was the one, already well known to me as Jim, freshly presented in his annotated copies of the novels and non-fiction, and the other of a different order altogether from the author I'd met as teenager in 'Introduction to the Novel 101'. For when I inherited Jim's library and turned myself over to the business of organising it – selecting, after his family had seen them all, those books I and others who loved Jim would keep, and those I would arrange into a library colleagues and students could also access – I saw then how much of Jim's library was all of his James.

Even as I write all this – and indeed how much more there is to write and how I could go on! Now that Henry James has given me licence to exercise my prior predilection for the free and happy use of the exclamation mark, even, how I could go on, and on! – I see how my syntax, as a result of the Jamesian submersion of these past months, has quickened my own means of expression, that I might now justify certain aspects of my own go at prose; with these novels as my guide feel more free about the idiosyncratic and cryptic – and to allow, through the sure and sturdy establishment of precedent, a goodly number of associated subordinate clauses of my own devising, that they too may come out to show themselves in the fine air. 'How much of Jim's library was all of his James', indeed. Reading all the Henry James has done this to me; it's formed an authorisation of certain effects – for particular punctuation or arrangement of phrase, for the peculiarly expressed or jumpy quirk. That 'morsel of court plaster'. The gorgeous link up of 'apparent incongruities of a taste for housework and the wearing of fresh Parisian-looking dresses suggested the possession of a dangerous energy'. Heaven. Heaven, heaven. I've already forgotten who is being talked about here, what is happening in this chapter or to whom, but goodness I remember the sentences, the tone of them, the sound, the make-up of their paste, the taste. It's as though I've been given my own version of 'Tradition and the Individual Talent', some ballast and a hearty sense of masterly heft to stand at the back of my own hazarding thumps at novels, to push me on. This, 'by the art of figuring synthetically, a compactness into which the imagination may cut thick, as into the rich density of wedding-cake', is how James himself put it. Compactness indeed. Before my year's study I might have thought my love of italics, say – as a way of going back to a thing in a story, an idea or an image, and bringing it out again to resonate, or simply to use the same thing, over and over, and move its context slightly, in the process – I might have thought that was a little something I simply enjoyed, for its own sake. Now I see it all comes from undergraduate reading of Henry James's novels that must have soaked in, even while a grumpy and opinionated teenager, and altered my literary temperament. 'As I altered my syntax I altered my intellect', wrote Yeats. Well, that must have started for me with Isabel Archer and Merton Densher. While I was throwing *The Wings of the Dove* across the room and longing to get back to William Carlos Williams there was James, wheedling his way into my imagination, making his ideas things in his own fastidious novelistic fashion and creating word field after field, his very own mightily turning and whirling machines of nouns, verbs and adjectives. And though I'd been playing and playing, one might say, in the past – to return to the musical metaphor with which I began this essay – at reading those novels and always stopping, starting – and then having to go back, back, back to the beginning, rap-a-tat-tat, and in a poor and halt fashion finally getting to the end... Even though there was all that monkey business of me never much caring for James... I now see, having all Jim's books to hand, his carefully annotated novels and underlinings in the two big volumes about method, that what Jim was trying to point me to, those years ago when he was still alive and I had started *Caroline's Bikini*, the project of mine I wanted to be entirely about the making of a thing in words, was that James was always going to be one who would show me how.

In a book just out, *Imitating Authors: Plato to Futurity*, the critic and scholar Colin Burrow talks about the way literature easily and naturally runs out into the ink of anyone who writes. We just can't help it, he says. Whatever one might think of Eliot, and Eliotian views of the tradition of literature, and irrespective of Eliot's own quite wilful and obvious adoption of past methods and approaches as a way of grafting literary heft on to his musings, there is much to be gained from simply acknowledging the amount of others' listed and unlisted stores in our own work, Burrows reminds us: '"Imitation" is an important concept because it is one which has never been completely broken down into its constituent elements'. No good believing all Harold Bloom says about belatedness, he tells us; you can never miss a good thing. The party is going on and on – it always has – and all of us are invited.

During those piano lessons in the dark – and also, for that matter, conducted in the spring and summer when it was light and getting warmer – my mother would wait for me in the car before taking me on to school. I look back and wonder what she was thinking of – about the whole thing? Five years old, six years old... Seven thirty in the morning, winter, spring, summer and autumn and still I couldn't play 'March of the Tin Soldiers' without breaking down into – my father has a tape recording of this, some thirteen versions in all which still reduces him to tears of laughter – false starts, botched beginnings, tense near-the-end misses and thoroughly awkward stops and mistakes all set to the sound of my repeated, crestfallen 'oh'.

The 'oh' meant the ruler, of course. 'You keep making mistakes and then grunting, oh,' I remember quite clearly the unkind piano teacher saying – the worst thing, that remark, 'grunting', about those lessons. Worse by far the word than the actual rap. By then no amount of fancy nail polish was going to make me believe she was worth sticking at. My mother finally took the advice of my aunt who was a professional classical musician to send me to another piano teacher and the sense of relief was as though all the summer holidays had arrived at once. Mrs Dickson, coincidentally, lived in the same street as the other one – the same street to which my own family moved when I was nine. She lived at the next house along. For half a year I'd had to walk down the road for a sharp early morning lesson in Bach. Now, 'such bliss was it in that dawn to be alive', it wasn't dawn at all, lessons were scheduled after school and I only needed, as my mother said, to 'pop next door'.

That phrase I've just used is all gathered up in my fully embraced telling about the writing of Henry James. A 'pop next door' in another time and context might have appealed to him too, I like to think – the effervescent after-school ease with which I might just 'pop' into my newly arranged and wonderfully productive lessons where the beneficent Mrs Dickson (I love her still) saw at once that it was my maths – or lack of -- that might be the thing and put me straight on to the Impressionists. I was off! Debussy. Ravel. Those rapturous Chopin Nocturnes and Impromptus. And as I draw to the end of my playing, an essay theme emerging whole around which I have arranged my thoughts on an author I now love, I shall take my leave at those smoothly managed lessons of my later childhood where all was pleasantly 'pop next door' and where I learned, on instruction, that the way to understand, to get to, the heart of a piece and then be able to perform it in full was to play it through – don't worry about the stumblings or uncertainty or of the difficulty of some of the bars or phrases – but slowly. Slowly first, so you get the sense of an overall approach and sense and shape. Then, after a few turns, the playing will get faster and faster, all of the separate notes coming together, one after the other, and getting better and better all the way through to the end – and then, somehow, brava! You have the thing in hand.

'He Takes Leave of the Sea' and Other Poems

Shane McCrae

Reading Is on Your List of Chores

The world is wild and sad, you're wild and sad
Daughter, and you want only, but you on-
ly want to watch the shows you want
To watch, the worlds you want to watch, to be allowed
To not be told the world
Is none of the worlds you're watching, none
Of the any worlds that would allow at an-
y moment you to rise and walk away, is none of the worlds you could

Turn from, your head away, by
Leaving it tame it, though it borrows wildness from your fear
And we have told you *No*
I have, your mother has, *Stay here*
To read with us, that we will help you understand here, from which you can't go
That understanding is not taming

He Takes Leave of the Sea

Some work I left undone, angers, the sea
That will not get a mention on my stone
Some work. Rattles its chain, loved and alone
Its cane, as one who was loved not enough, but lastingly

And broken since their sense of what love ought
To be, great sorrow of the empty house
And in, and lasts. The poem of the loss
Is a whole life of poems, and so gets longer as it short-

ens. I have walked away from the sea, and felt
The sea as if it were a cape or train
It doesn't pull me back, but drags behind
Me as I go, heavy as sorrow, long as it is to tell

Melissa at Her Desk

When I to bed, Melissa to her office
Go, then she goes, Melissa to her work
Her office and her work at the gray desk
Five feet from me, a world, a wall four inches

Thick and a world of silence in the wall
Sky-gray, surrounded by blue paintings, high
On the three walls nearest her, the gray desk sky-
Gray, the walls white as high white clouds. I pull

The sea-blue comforter with stars on it
Over my face. Stars wait on the sea-blue sea
Melissa to the night-blue chair

And dream. The stars then between us ignite
And burn on the other side of the comforter
Melissa sits on the night-blue chair like night on the sea

Borderline Ghazal

Reem Abbas

I swore I told no body
but swearing holds no body.

This body holds fast somehow
exile patrols nobody.

Beholden, believed body
you touched, held cold no body.

Leave me hang, I am no suspect
bare for all this holed know body.

Blue is the name you give death
fine lies behold no body.

Sounding BREAK BAT BEAT commands:
peel eyes, bleed, blindfold no body.

Peace, body, peace; in death burn
to blue, gold for nobody.

What does it mean: philistine?
Qasida controls nobody.

Will not – can not be bul –
lied – bullshit sold no body.

CAT D9: the border is
breached leaks bold to gnaw body.

You wore the day gold on words
I broke the way you felled words.

Bodies batted like lashes
martyred, matted black like words.

Dizzy with swearing, I lied
peeled truth, blinded, bled true words.

Look: a tapestry hung on teeth!
A bulldozer, body of words!

How is it said: فلسطين?
Border line alive in words.

Found the sounds that made me sing:
words on the wing: winding in words.

Say peace: piece. Say hand: land. I
shake in body broke in words.

This counter qasida is
blue, freedom follows death in words.

To nought a body – will not
O no   a O   – knot in words.

Denied entry a gazelle
escapes, leaps like no words.

Palestine (filasṭīn)

'Ghazal' (غزل) in Arabic means both to speak amorous sayings and to wind thread around a spindle. Where the subject matter of ghazals often praises the beloved, its mechanism resembles the intimate act of winding. Wool/words spin around the wood/form to make an intentional, compact ball of yarn. Threads twist around each other, wool winds tightly around a core, repeating and repeating itself to conclusion/sound.

Amongst the earliest British translators of the Arabo-Persian ghazal are James Mangan and Gertrude Bell, both of whose complex relationships with 'the Orient' gave rise to equally complex and rich translations. As more of Hafez's ghazals became available, anglophone interest in Eastern poetry evolved into an interest in the poetic form itself. Alfred Tennyson, James Elroy Flecker and Thomas Hardy are but a few poets who would later adapt and subsume the form into their own work. Across the Atlantic, the ghazal only became a mainstream form in 1970 when Aijaz Ahmad edited a small anthology entitled *Ghazals of Ghalib: Versions from the Urdu* (1994). He collaborated with seven contemporaneous American poets – including Adrienne Rich, Mark Strand, and William Hunt – to translate thirty-seven of Ghalib's ghazals into English. Ahmad's version of the English ghazal forfeited its formal constraints in favor of an essential and purely thematic approach. In response to this, Agha Shahid Ali came out with an edited collection of ghazals entitled *Ravishing DisUnities: Real Ghazals in English* (2000). In the introduction, Shahid Ali outlined the form's strictures and contextualised it within an Urdu linguistic and geographical context in which the ghazal form is intimately tied to its performance. Ghazals are often read at *mushairas*, where the poem's refrain is repeated back to the poet by the audience in ecstatic anticipation. The ghazal's internal formal tensions thus became tied with tensions in translation across languages and cultures, which then gave rise to tensions of a perfectly (un)broken English ghazal. This triple poetic axis is complicated constantly by the contemporary ghazal poet's own personal and literary context.

My ghazal, its wood and wool, came in a rare Wordsworthian overflow of poetic emotion after having read the news. I was at the time writing an essay on the excesses of the English ghazal which encouraged me to attempt to express a winding excess of my own.

System and Agon

Nicolas Tredell

Harold Bloom, *Take Arms Against a Sea of Troubles: The Power of the Reader's Mind over a Universe of Death* (Yale University Press) £25

Like Los in William Blake's *Jerusalem*, Harold Bloom, who died on 14 October 2019 at the age of eighty-nine, might have said, in terms of his critical career, 'I must Create a System or be enslav'd by another Man's'. In his prolific criticism, he did create a rich system elaborated around the idea of what the title of his 1973 book called 'the anxiety of influence', the supposed struggle of 'strong' poets with their precursors and the complex stratagems they employed to try to achieve their poetic and personal individuation. This system, while sometimes tending towards the scholastic, remains fascinating in its intricacy and its insights, even if the latter are sometimes blurred as Bloom often stayed at two removes from the textual minutiae on which the crucial techne of twentieth-century literary criticism, close reading, characteristically focuses.

Bloom's system enabled him both to avoid the piecemeal empiricism of a fragmenting New Criticism and to remain independent of structuralism, deconstruction and post-structuralism, in contrast to his sometime Yale colleagues J. Hillis Miller and Geoffrey Hartman – the latter a close friend whom, in a 1987 interview with Imre Salusinszky, Bloom called 'the largest single American casualty of Jacques [Derrida] and Paul [de Man]'. While it may have been unfair to consign later Hartman to the casualty ward, Bloom never risked any such fate because he had his own system – 'theory' is not quite the right word for it, even if it has some convergences with the theoretical perspectives that came to the USA from Europe. His later excursions into critical populism and polemicism, in *The Western Canon* (1994; reviewed *PNR* 104) and *Shakespeare: The Invention of the Human* (1998), were less happy, but towards the end of his career he returned to a more esoteric and elitist mode – and 'elitist' here should not be understood as pejorative, as it is in current populist political discourse; Bloom himself declared, in that 1987 interview: 'Elitism is the condition of the spirit'. This posthumous work continues in that mode.

The subtitle of *Take Arms Against a Sea of Troubles* announces the book's main premise: *The Power of the Reader's Mind over a Universe of Death*. This is adapted from a passage in Frank Kermode's *Wallace Stevens* (1960) that Bloom quotes later in the book and the phrase 'a universe of death' is (although Bloom does not say this) from the conclusion to Wordsworth's *The Prelude* in both the 1805 and 1850 versions. This layering of references is characteristic of Bloom's approach but his subtitle also seems to move, in what is perhaps a last populist gesture on his part, into the realm of the self-help manual and bibliotherapy. In the early pages of the book, he declares: 'The mind is an activity and will decay into dark inertia if not sustained by the sustenance of reading'.

Like Bloom's previous book, *The Daemon Knows* (2015; reviewed *PNR* 2016), *Take Arms* has faults. It may have undergone some editing before publication, but if so, it could have done with more. Most of the quotations are much longer than they need to be to demonstrate the points Bloom makes, so that the book sometimes seems like an erratic anthology interspersed with eccentric commentaries rather than a work of literary criticism in any conventional sense. There is a tendency to change tack in mid-paragraph that sometimes recalls, unkindly, the sentence with which Steinbeck sums up the abrupt mental shifts of Grampa Joad in *The Grapes of Wrath*: 'His mind jumped'. But if the ends of Bloom's paragraphs sometimes forget their beginnings, we should resist the temptation to adopt the patronizing tone of Regan to King Lear: 'O sir, you are old…'. The author of this book was indeed old, nearly ninety, and made no secret of the fact; indeed there is a strand in *Take Arms* that we could index under the title of one of Christine Brooke-Rose's final works: *Life, End of* (2006): we hear, for instance, of his falls, his knee pains, his insomnia, his dictating from a hospital chair or bed (this last perhaps partly accounts for its jump-cuts within paragraphs). But even if not quite in his perfect mind, he has not lost his wits.

Take Arms might have been better, however, if Bloom had been bold enough to break free of what comes across, at this stage in his work, as the tyranny of the paragraph. His jump-cut prose constantly tends towards the condition of aphorism, and a Blakean, Nietzchean or even Wildean aphoristic mode might have been better suited to his manner of interpretation and to his difficulty with following through an argument. Bloom was never primarily a close reader in the manner of, say, early Empson, but an intuitive interpreter; his approach is perhaps best summed up by his description, in this book, of a particular kind of difficulty with Hart Crane's poetry, who 'pitches his tone so high that the reader can be left behind, unable to keep up with the leap of a "logic of metaphor" storming the heights of the Unapparent'. Bloom's own critical leaps can yield insights invisible to readers who get so close to the text they lose apprehension of the whole, like viewers who gets too near an Impressionist painting. But they can also seem like examples of a '[v]aulting ambition which o'erleaps itself / And falls on th'other'. Their scope is also constrained by having to accommodate to the critical subgenre that Bloom's system entails, the psychodrama, sometimes swelling into melodrama, of 'the anxiety of influence' in which strong poets are seen as struggling against powerful precursors. This psychodrama promotes an endless displacement of one poet's corpus into the corpora of prior poets (in Bloom's perspective, only Shakespeare escapes this by becoming his own precursor); it turns a poem into a portal that allows access to another portal and then another, a series of dissolving views that never stay still long enough to acquire a solid existence in their own right. Of course, poems always emerge from a matrix of other poems; but a poem of any power takes on an existence of its own, as New Criticism at its best emphasised. One of the precursors of New Criticism is Matthew Arnold, second only to T. S. Eliot in Bloom's menagerie of *bêtes noires*; but Arnold's idea, formulated in 'On Translating Homer' (1861) and repeated in 'The Function of Criticism at the Present Time' (1864), that criticism should strive '[t]o see the object as in itself it really is' remains a touchstone of good critical practice, despite or possibly because of the epistemological and ontological difficulties, even perhaps impossibilities, of such whole and steady vision.

The coverage of canonical English and American poets in *Take Arms* includes Dante, Shakespeare, Milton, Blake, Wordsworth, Keats, Shelley, Byron, Browning, Tennyson, Whitman, Frost, Stevens, Yeats, and Hart Crane. Freud also features, whose scientific claims Bloom dismisses but whom, he tells us, he reads and rereads as he does Montaigne or Cervantes or Shakespeare. If twenty-first-century etiquette prompts the observation that this is an all-male line-up, it is not primarily in the interests of the non-literary criterion of gender balance that one would like to see Bloom addressing the work of more female poets; it is, rather, because one would like to hear what he has to say about them, beyond the polemical denigration that sometimes mars his work; Emily Dickinson has some honourable mentions but it would be interesting, in the context this book creates, to have his take on, for example, Adrienne Rich, a poet steeped in tradition but striking out on her own – think of the differences (and continuities) between, say, 'Vertigo' and 'Diving into the Wreck'.

Bloom does, however, consider two less well-publicised male poets, one of them an African American. The first, briefly but poignantly discussed, is Trumbull Stickney, whose work, like that of the early Wallace Stevens, seems to Bloom 'a kind of American pre-Raphaelitism' – he quotes 'Mnesoyme' and 'On Some Shells Found Inland' – and who, Bloom feels, 'could have come close to Wallace Stevens in achievement' but for his early death at the age of thirty. The second, more extensively considered, is Jay Wright, now eighty-five, whom Bloom considered 'the best living American poet' since the departure of 'John Ashbery and his generation'. Bloom identifies 'a foundation stone' of Wright's 'ambitious edifice' as the 'wry realization of the otherness of black history' and sees the 'central figuration in his poetry' as 'creation-by-twinning, a myth of divine creation in West African Dogon mythology'. Wright's 'major mode' is 'his own modification of the Pindaric ode'.

Bloom's intuitive interpretative leaps are only one aspect of this book. Old men forget, but the lighted rooms inside their heads can suddenly glow into vivid vignettes of the past. One of the most engaging elements of *Take Arms* is its memories of fellow critics Bloom has known – or, at least in one notable case, not got to know: this was in Cambridge, England, in 1954 when Bloom was a Fulbright Scholar at Pembroke College:

> my adviser (who became a lifelong friend) Matthew Hodgart took me to tea with F. R. Leavis and his wife, Queenie. Soon after we were seated, Dr. Leavis asked me what the subject of my Yale doctoral dissertation-in-progress was. I answered: 'Shelley.' Dr. Leavis responded: 'I have settled Shelley.' At twenty-four I was rather brash and replied: 'Shelley always buries his own undertakers.' My host jumped up and left the room. His wife made a speechless gesture indicating that Hodgart and I were to depart, without taking tea. Matthew and I walked over to the Anchor pub and substituted Highland malt for tea and sausages for teacake.

The anecdote reflects badly on Leavis but is consistent with other examples of his behaviour in the post-war era towards those who disagreed with him (even former disciples like L. C. Knights). It is also a harbinger of one of Bloom's achievements: his contribution to the rehabilitation of Shelley, and more generally of certain styles of Romanticism, after Leavis and Eliot had, to use the 1930s verb, dislodged them.

If no dialogue with Leavis was possible, or later, with Cleanth Brooks, 'with whom I never had a civil exchange', Bloom did maintain dialogues with a range of other critics. For example, he admired Empson's *Milton's God* (1961) and reread it when he started to write *The Anxiety of Influence*. In *Take Arms*, he recalls their first meeting at Yale:

> When we were introduced, he said, 'You are the man who wrote that dotty book on influence. I like dotty books.' I expressed my admiration for his work as a critic and for his sparse but splendid achievement as a poet. He had been reading Hart Crane and wanted to talk about the *Voyages*, where we found deep agreement. Sharing his championship of Shelley, we went on to an exchange on the relationship between Crane and Shelley.

One would like to have eavesdropped on that conversation.

Perhaps the most intriguing friendship recollected in *Take Arms* is with Paul de Man, to whom Bloom felt close despite their significant critical disagreements and to whose memory he stayed loyal even after the posthumous revelation of de Man's wartime writings. At one point, Bloom observes: 'I understand that Paul struggled inwardly with those dark years in occupied Belgium when he wrote so many collaborationist articles, including at least one that is anti-Semitic', and he goes on to suggest: 'Only in retrospect can I now apprehend that on more than one occasion he attempted to talk to me about this. Since I had no idea what he could have meant except perhaps Flemish nationalism, I never encouraged him to say more'. The idea that de Man might have been engaged in an intense inner struggle and seen Bloom as a privileged confidante is dramatic but dubious; in post-war Yale, de Man gave scant sign that he was guilt-haunted and seems to have behaved more like a character in a le Carré novel, a secret agent who has infiltrated an enemy institution and is constantly on guard lest his cover gets blown. Bloom's observations, however, are further testimony of de Man's remarkable capacity, which seems to have been at least partly that of a confidence trickster, to inspire friendship and after his death, when the worst was revealed, to generate apologias. Perhaps Bloom's tolerance was also due, on some level, to an awareness of aspects of his own past behaviour that might incur opprobrium today.

Bloom's soft-pedalling on de Man's anti-semitism contrasts markedly with his attitude to T. S. Eliot. The 'abominable Eliot', as he calls him in *Take Arms*, was Bloom's biggest *bête noire*. Eliot's anti-semitism certainly played its part in this; Bloom, while finding Freud's *The Future of an Illusion* (1927) possibly 'his weakest book', relished 'the image of T. S. Eliot, respectable anti-Semite, reading it in a fury'. Bloom also disliked what he called Eliot's 'vehement dogmatism', comparing his denunciation of D. H. Lawrence in *After Strange Gods* (1934) to 'John Calvin burning Michael Servetus at the stake in Geneva on October 27, 1553'. He further deplored 'his misogyny' and 'his lasting contempt for human nature'. But Bloom's animus seems to exceed the necessary reprobation of such flaws. One passage in *Take Arms* perhaps gives a clue to one reason for it: 'Eliot still has his admirers, though mostly for the best of his poems, and not for his critical and polemical prose'. Clearly Bloom here relishes the thought that Eliot has apparently now been dislodged, as Eliot and Leavis once dislodged Shelley. But it is significant that he focuses especially on a perceived waning of admiration for Eliot's 'critical and polemical prose' – precisely the areas in which Bloom sought to establish himself throughout his long and copious career. Might not the exorbitance of his anti-Eliotism be a case of the anxiety of influence, the desire to defeat and triumph over a precursor critic, overwhelmingly influential when Bloom first came to Yale? Bloom does not seem to ask himself this question; perhaps another reason for his aversion to Matthew Arnold is that he seems incapable of that 'return ... upon himself' that Arnold, in 'The Function of Criticism at the Present Time', so admired in Burke.

The Waste Land suggests two further reasons for Bloom's aversion to Eliot. This great Modernist poem presents a peculiarly strong threat to Bloom's system, his psychodrama/melodrama of influence. In *Take Arms*, Bloom tries to fit *The Waste Land* into it by claiming that it 'can be viewed primarily as a revision of Walt Whitman's "Lilacs" elegy, which in one sense it most certainly is'. Despite Bloom's qualifying phrase 'in one sense', this seems like a loosely associative comparison flimsily based on the '[l]ilacs out of the dead land' in the poem's second line and resembles some of the examples of inaccurate reading in I. A. Richards's protocols in *Practical Criticism* (1929). Bloom also attempts generic definitions that shade into banal autobiographical readings: '*The Waste Land* essentially is an elegy both for Jean Verdenal ['*mort aux Dardanelles*'] and for Eliot himself'. But the range of references to past literature in *The Waste Land* makes it peculiarly difficult to isolate distinctive agons with precursors, even with Shakespeare because, in a sense, the poem is upfront about its appropriations. In a famous affirmation in his 1921 essay on Philip Massinger, Eliot does not deny the possibility of an adversarial relationship between past and present poets but, unlike Bloom, he does not locate it in what *Finnegans Wake* called 'the penumbra of the procuring room', that gloomy sub-Freudian basement in which Bloom confines his poets. Rather, in his formulation of a strong poet's relationship to his predecessors, he implicitly invokes not Hades but Hermes, quicksilver god of thieves: 'Immature poets imitate; mature poets steal; bad poets deface what they take, and good poets make it into something better, or at least something different'. In a sense, this is a nutshell anticipation of Bloom's notion of agonistic influence; but it brings it into the light and does not suggest that it is the only possible relationship between past and present poets.

The second challenge to Bloom's system that *The Waste Land* presents is that the agon of the poem (not to be conflated, as Bloom casually does, with Eliot's personal struggles) is not primarily with past poets but with the present in which it was written – with what Eliot called, in his 1923 essay on the 'mythical method' of Joyce's *Ulysses*, 'the immense panorama of futility and anarchy which is contemporary history'. The main quest of the poem is, as Samuel Beckett later said more generally of the task of the twentieth-century artist, 'to find a form that accommodates the mess' (and this formal search may reveal that the apparent mess springs from a misperception). A poem is responsible to its present even as it steals from, struggles with, or graciously relates to the poems and other cultural forms of the past. It is this last possibility, of a gracious relation, which Bloom ignores. Must the relationship between poet and precursors always be exclusively agonistic? Surely this is only one aspect of a complex interaction that may also involve homage, tribute, fruitful continuity? If, following Bloom's system and applying it to critics, we look at his relationship with Eliot as an agon, he is the loser; Old Possum still beats Old Bloom. But in the more capacious view of the dynamics of poetic creation that Eliot offers, Bloom's account has a distinctive though circumscribed place.

'Raptor' and Other Poems

RICHARD HOFFMAN

Kyrie

10 31 2020

Samhain, and a Blue Moon's near red Mars.
The days grow shorter and more hard hours
   are added to our nights.
The angel of history feels useless; she told me
in a nightmare filled with the pornography
   of sadness and its delights.
Sing kyrie, sing kyrie eleison;
none of us should suffer this darkness alone.

Foundlings on earth, from hell or heaven,
at night our shadows show us what will happen,
   and in the morning, rising,
we become again their vital obstruction.
Who abandoned us is a useless question
   unworthy of all the arguing.
Sing kyrie, sing kyrie eleison:
May all earth's deadly resentments be done.

The wind picks up and whistles in the woods.
Days pass fast as breaks in hastened clouds.
   The angel of history shrugs
and throws up her hands, 'I told you so!'
but what it was she told we'll never know;
   she speaks in tongues.
Sing kyrie, sing kyrie eleison:
Restore our terrifying human minds to reason.

Raptor

A silhouette, mostly, in clear October sky.
A goshawk maybe, or a broad-winged,
I'd have to see it again; I can only tell you
I heard its cry and felt its gaze, a laser,
before I passed beneath the aging trees
and kept on, walking and thinking all day.
At dusk the lamps along the path came on,
and lit the leaves a bright unnatural colour.
I never knew trees that seemed to worry
so much about what they might say to me
as those along the paved walk out of there:
To be truthful is to remember and grieve.
Then headlights, tail lights, highway, night,
a few clouds passing a half moon, stars.

Contrast

What if this moment is the opposite
of the change to colour in Wizard of Oz? —
B&W now making things explicit,

requiring us to choose, to commit.
What if there is no escape because
this is that moment? Is the opposite

of dazzling colour clarifying spirit?
Can we re-evaluate all that was?
B&W now making things explicit,

we see the old footage, counterfeit
and colorised, and grasp what it does.
What if this moment is the opposite

of cant and evasion and bullshit,
of any and all the pastel nostalgias,
B&W now making things explicit

so we're finally freed from our habit
of dressing abuse in colourful disguises?
What if this moment is the opposite,
B&W now making things explicit?

Two Poems

THOMAS McCARTHY

From Salonica

The bulky Famine ship that came over the sea was a fork

And never a spoon. The sea couldn't be bothered.
The shore was a surprise of place settings
Neatly arranged, the moist food ample

And nourishing, the *Ajax* sailing for Bristol,
Sixty boxes of salmon, three hundred lambs aboard.
Inbound, the *Iona* from Philadelphia,
Wanting to be part of our story, a berth in the pageant

That would go on and on. Sugar from Trinidad

For our betters in the city, the *Kaffirland*
With guano, the *Aurora* with Bangor manure.
The *Lizzie Anne* for Alexandria, *Seagull* from Odessa;

And from Salonica, the *Flying Cloud*.
Something miraculous in the continuity of trade,
As miraculous as the way we're still upset
With deaths in unmarked famine graves. But what

Was a captain to do, or a shipping agent,

When the unchartered died beneath their wake?
Such plenty as the sea has, such a plenitude of trade,
Is only in the keeping going between a chosen few,

The chosen who come aboard this ship of a poem,
Its cargo discharged, it lyric intent;
Aboard as a chandler at high tide on the south jetty,
Rum in his full decanter: his laden bulk, his behemoth.

An Old-Fashioned

I was sitting there in the older *Shelbourne* Bar
With my daughter, Kate Inez,
Drinking the most flagrant if not fragrant
Cocktail in the whole universe,

When a man walked in and offered me
A distributor's licence for *Waterford Glass*.
Be careful what you long for, my daughter said:
She is wise like her mother. But my dreams

Seemed to come true at that moment;
And the greatest dream of all, to handle
Only the finest crystal: I would go to the end
Of my days handling only the *Lismore* suite.

As the ice melted in the bourbon glass
I thought of all the idiots Prince Myshkin met
In Dostoevsky's book; disillusioned
Soldiers, drunk and despondent lords,

The truly demented at each border station. I thought:
I've made poems for all of them, for years.
Why shouldn't I celebrate a great craft now –
With a steady hand, the positively good in glass?

Intimate Distance: Robert Giroux & John Berryman

TONY ROBERTS

'Every good thing that comes is accompanied by trouble' is a line attributed to the legendary editor of Fitzgerald, Hemingway and Wolfe, Max Perkins. It is particularly applicable to the dealings of another great editor, Robert Giroux, with his client John Berryman.

Readers are familiar with Berryman's fêted yet frantic life – the brilliance, the destructive alcoholism, the manic depression, the periodic infatuation with suicide – and especially with the idiolect of his *Dream Songs* protagonist. We may not be as familiar with Giroux, whose talent took him from a modest background into the, then, country-club world of publishing, where he eventually became the third partner at Farrar, Straus, founded in 1946. With unfailing admiration, patience and encouragement, he was to edit over a dozen books by the poet.

The two met in Mark Van Doren's Shakespeare class at Columbia University in the early 1930s. Van Doren, a Pulitzer Prize winning poet ('the great teacher in my life', according to Giroux), was admired for his 'technique of pretending that you were his intellectual equal'. Berryman remained equally impressed: 'It was the force of his example that made me a poet'. Giroux came under another influence also, that of biographer and editor Raymond Weaver who had helped pluck Melville from posthumous obscurity. Their serious commitment to study helped the two students cement a friendship, that and *The Columbia Review*, which Giroux co-edited and where Berryman published poems and reviews.

After Columbia, Berryman won a scholarship to Clare College, Cambridge, at which time he heard Eliot and met Yeats and Dylan Thomas. Greatly influenced by the example of Yeats and the behaviour of Thomas, he was there at the latter's death in New York. 'He was my oldest friend still a friend, except Giroux', he wrote, 'but not personally close for many years'.

He went on to teach at various universities: Wayne State, Harvard, Princeton (where his friend, Saul Bellow, remembered him as 'tallish, slender, nervous, and [giving] many signs that he was inhibiting erratic impulses'), Washington, Cincinnati, and then at the University of Minnesota from 1955 until his death. Contributing to Berryman's lifelong instability were his parents. Giroux described 'Jill' Berryman as 'a campus mother who haunted him daily, from his undergraduate days at John Jay Hall to his wintertime suicide in Minneapolis in 1972'. Worse had been the impact of his father's suicide: 'The shadow of my father's shaming death / lay over a youth. / Phantoms suckt at my chances'.

Although a keen Shakespeare scholar, Berryman's energies were directed principally to poetry and teaching. Demanding and extremely popular as a teacher – his students included the poets Justice, Levine and Snodgrass – he frequently exhausted himself. On one occasion in April 1957 he wrote to Giroux, 'One very fatiguing thing is that my modern course has so jammed with people that every morning at 11:30 I talk to 104 students. My department has never had anything like this before, and I can do it all right, but it is a strain.' Like his friend Lowell, in dark times he might journey from hospital to classroom and back.

On leaving Columbia, Giroux turned first to public relations. He had excelled at school but with the Depression dropped out to work on a local newspaper, 'The Jersey Journal'. With the editor's advocacy he won a scholarship to Columbia, there changing from journalism to literature. After graduation he first joined CBS, before being taken on as a junior editor with Harcourt, Brace & Company. The famously finicky Edmund Wilson was an early client – and very lightly edited.

Enlisting in the US Navy in 1942, Giroux served as a combat intelligence officer on the USS *Essex*. In action he witnessed the rescue of a fighter pilot at the battle of Truk Lagoon in the Pacific and took his account at the war's end to the US Navy Information Office in New York, where Roger Straus worked. Straus sold his story to 'Collier's' for 1,000 dollars. It was to be a doubly productive meeting since Straus would eventually need just the literary talents Giroux had to offer.

Meanwhile the latter returned to Harcourt, Brace, rising to the position of executive editor, where he published the early work of Lowell, Flannery O'Connor and Bernard Malamud. Eventually, frustrations with senior colleagues, especially after facing their indifference to his work on Orwell, E. E. Cummings and William Gaddis *and* losing both *Catcher in the Rye* and *On the Road*, caused Giroux to look for more independence. Roger Straus coaxed him to Farrar, Straus in 1955.

The story of F.S.G., as it was to become – with its famous three-fish colophon – is entertainingly told in *Hothouse* (2013), by Boris Kachka. With reluctant family support, the extrovert Straus bought his way into publishing by taking as a partner the veteran John Farrar. Farrar, Straus survived on a catalogue that produced the odd surprise hit (like *Look Younger, Live Longer*, the nation's bestseller in 1950). Straus, however, looked to a niche that would bring them literary respectability in the market. One ploy was to enlist admired, if slow-selling writers (Wilson, Trilling, Van Doren) to serve as decoys for upmarket authors.

Hiring Giroux proved a master stroke. He possessed excellent taste. He also brought twenty writers over to F. S. with him, including T. S. Eliot (now a personal friend) and Lowell and his circle. It was generally conceded that Giroux would go to lengths to protect his writers, visiting them in distress (Lowell during a manic cycle; working with Jean Stafford's aphasia) and his enthusiasm proved endearing. He prided himself on being an editor in close collaboration with his writers.

In 1964 his reward came as a partnership, with Lowell's

For the Union Dead the first collection issued under the new imprint Farrar, Straus and Giroux. The company, braced by Straus's extension of their international list, would eventually include eighteen Nobel Prize winners (among them Brodsky, Miłosz, Heaney and Walcott), becoming the primary mid-size literary publisher in America.

Long before that, John Berryman had re-entered Giroux's life. Their relationship is captured in all its convolutions in the fascinating *John Berryman and Robert Giroux: A Publishing Friendship by* Patrick Samway, S. J. (University of Notre Dame Press, 2020). The dramatic kernel in Samway's book relates to the friends' divergent paths after Columbia. The Kellett Fellowship that sent Berryman to Cambridge had been offered first to Giroux – thanks to Van Doren – though without certain details that would prompt him to accept it. He came to resent both Van Doren and Berryman since, according to Samway, he 'had a deep-seated secret desire to surpass the essays written about Shakespeare' by the two of them. Samway, who later knew Giroux well, writes, '"It doesn't matter now," he once told me, "but it mattered a good deal then."' A consummate professional, Giroux kept emotional distance within these intimacies.

In June 1940 Berryman pitched Giroux the idea of a solo collection with Harcourt, Brace. He explained he was keen to evade a commitment of twenty poems to James Laughlin's New Directions anthology *Five Young American Poets*: 'I have never much liked the idea… it took Schwartz, Tate and Van Doren a month to persuade me'. Giroux replied that he would try to publish it, though he had anticipated another book they discussed in New York. Berryman had projected a prose work, a Blitz record of 'the death of our kind of life'. It had been partly a romantic scheme of his to return to England and his 'Beatrice' of 1937.

Giroux recommended Berryman pursue the Laughlin offer, knowing that during wartime it would be impossible for poets without a reputation to be published. Otherwise, he assured the poet, 'I'm ready to battle for you to the bitter end. I'm delighted to; it will be the first occasion since I've been here that I really want to see a book published'. Testament to their friendship: Giroux had been asked to be best man when Berryman married Eileen Mulligan in October 1942. When he could not obtain leave from his naval posting at Norfolk, Virginia, Van Doren took his place.

Berryman daringly turned down Giroux's offer to publish his first collection, *The Dispossessed* (1948), maintaining a commitment to William Sloane Associates. Fortunately, when Giroux joined Straus he wanted to build up their American list and so approached Berryman about *Homage to Mistress Bradstreet*, his powerful, idiosyncratic take on the Colonial American poet: 'I can now sign contracts myself, and there will be none of the Harcourt, Brace ambivalence'. Giroux apparently wanted his next four books, hinting at spring publication for *Bradstreet*.

Ultimately, he extracted Berryman from a Viking Press contract for a Shakespeare biography, repaying the advance given, plus offering a second $1,000 to Berryman for the *Bradstreet* collection and the (never-to-appear) Shakespeare. Habitually anxious about publishing, Berryman would soon turn wary in his correspondence with his friend. He ended one letter, 'I take it that the book is thought of now as coming out at once. This is what I very strongly want, for reasons that I'll tell you in a long letter immediately if you'll tell me immediately if this is what you <u>don't</u> plan. But if you do plan it, let me know too.'

In a copy signed to Giroux, Berryman inscribed the sentiment, 'w. admiration & affection', for rescuing the poet when 'dying, not in brain but in heart & spirit'. Unfortunately, the response of the literary world to *Bradstreet* proved disappointing, despite Giroux's efforts. By May 1958 things had soured. Berryman wrote complaining of the failure of Farrar, Straus to promote his book. He expressed bewilderment that copies of *Bradstreet* were unavailable, citing complaints at various readings and publisher statements recording fewer than a hundred sales in six months. He pointed to a dearth of advertising for the book, repeated the critical fervour for it and questioned, 'what is businesslike and what is not'. The letter occasioned a rift between them.

Giroux, of course, had other clients to devote himself to. Between the winter of 1959 and through the following spring, for instance, he edited sixty-two books. Two years later Berryman attempted to heal the rift with a letter to Giroux's confidante, the editor Catharine Carver: 'Would you or will you make my peace with Robert? I wrote him an angry letter years ago. I shouldn't have done; though I felt even more justified when I saw an ad in some paper later that they were remaindering the Bradstreet poem for a buck,—I felt he shd have told me, and moreover I cd have bought some myself. Still I felt very bad abt the letter, not only personally (he is one of my oldest friends and I love him) but professionally'. He felt it had lowered his advance for the Shakespeare biography. He had more to say on the issue, he wrote, but his wife had pointed out, 'I got furious during the Giroux paragraph and I had better shut up'. (Straus had in fact remaindered *Bradstreet.*) Carver spoke to Giroux who said all Berryman had to do was drop him a note.

Encouraged at the prospect of reconciliation (and of publishing his *Dream Songs*), in February 1963 Berryman part-mended fences with Giroux in a characteristically see-sawing manner, 'Let's make an end of the long estrangement. I have felt bad about it a thousand times. I wrote you a letter I should not have sent; but then you did not reply at all, and perhaps that was going too far, too.' He recited again his grievance, before expressing eternal gratitude for Giroux's assistance in bringing his work to the public. There followed the Henry-like confession: 'still I feel puzzles and dissatisfactions about all that handling of it back there'. Here his self-pity flared momentarily with the feeling that despite the great merit recognised in his work, it had never had true publisher support. The letter ended with the demand for an offer for his *Dream Songs* and the accusation that he had never received anything for *Bradstreet*.

Giroux responded placatingly, 'I have never had any but the most affectionate feelings, arising from our most ancient and longstanding friendship' and, despite misunderstandings, 'I was deeply moved by your letter. Let us consider the long estrangement ended, though it never began for me.' 'Oh this is luxurious: thanks', Berryman replied.

That July he wrote again, feigning uncertainty about what to do with the Songs that continued to pour out. They were, he repeated, much admired by friends and journal editors (Tate, Wilson, Snodgrass, Spender, Alvarez were mentioned): 'I cannot decide... whether to sign with you, and give you 75 or whatever, or as many as 130, or 100 or so, or not to publish any now, I cannot decide'. He assured Giroux that he had signed to no other interested party (citing Stone Wall Press), but acknowledged that money worries and other projects pressed on him. 'Maybe the thing to do is stop exacerbating...', he wondered, and simply send them to Giroux, which he did.

Berryman revelled in the massive appreciation that greeted *77 Dream Songs*. At the same time, forever insecure, he remained critical of poor readings of them: 'I expected only the perfunctory from Allen [Tate] and so am not disapp't'd, but I could not foresee that both Cal [Lowell] and Mark [Van Doren] —in many words & in few—would wholly fail Henry'. Lowell had compounded the problem by reviewing the book: 'he does not understand it AT ALL—he thinks Henry is only 'one' of the characters and thinks Mr. Bones is distinct fr. H.' A permissible blunder, we might think, though not nearly as trying as the continuing eliding of poet and protagonist. (Lowell corrected his error by letter to the *NYRB*.)

Between the *Dream Songs* volumes, Giroux decided to publish *Berryman's Sonnets* (1967) – the product of an affair during his first marriage – with a $500 advance and another $500 on publication. Happy with the arrangement, Berryman indicated that the Songs continued to appear, 'some 40 in the last month alone'. When he came to organizing the second book of Songs, *His Toy, His Dream, His Rest* (1968), his editor reckoned 'the latter two books are longer than they should be'. In response Berryman removed four of six poems mentioned then – continuing to overflow – added two new ones.

Giroux's editorial role grew as Berryman's collapses increased in severity. Aside from tasks like ordering Songs, decoding scrambled letters and overseeing the 'unusually heavy revisions' Berryman would make close to publication, he had to pursue fees for granting permissions, carefully time the appearance of the abundant Songs to avoid overexposure, while finding other outlets ('Don't be surprised if you turn up in McCall's and Playboy'). It was vital to keep the momentum going, to bolster the poet's enthusiasm ('TOY DREAM REST IS SUPERB. YOUR GREATEST BOOK AND THAT IS SAYING A LOT') and to offer some clear idea of their publishing future, leading when Berryman flagged.

By late 1969 the poet reported a recent royalty cheque had brought him near $8,000 (approximately $70,000 today), whereas he had expected a mere £600. The following June he wrote to his mother about his latest venture: 'The book (Giroux thinks it "far & away yr best book" – wh. I don't agree with but am glad to hear) is called *Love & Fame* & it will make a sensation this Fall: though it may also (Mark thinks) be feared & hated'. Neither proved correct. Without his Henry, the confessional Berryman did not fare as well. But moving on, he reported to Giroux that 'Delusions' (*Delusions, Etc.*) would be the title of a subsequent collection, already containing about fifty poems. In June 1971 he asked for contracts for a novel, *Recovery*, and this collection, 'which is proceeding with slow confidence'. The slowness reflected his state of health; the completed book lacked the vitality of earlier work.

Berryman's last work in progress, the novel, would be published the year after his death. Having flown to Minneapolis to act as godfather for Berryman's second daughter in June 1971, Giroux read twenty-five pages of it while Berryman attended his AA meeting. The poet sweated with uncertainty, 'expecting to finally hear I shouldn't go on with it'. Yet Giroux proved encouraging, wrote Berryman, '"It's marvellous, John" & "Let's get a draft" & "What about ten thousand dollars" (advance, that is). Cosmic relief! After he left at 2 a.m., I felt faint & had to take a pain pill.'

Soon Giroux would be writing to a friend about Berryman's suicide, 'Having suffered so much and achieved so much, he had I thought finally reached some kind of balance and acceptance'. At the funeral he delivered a simple eulogy. Death would not be the editorial end, according to Kachka, 'There were [always] a thousand things to do: secure copyrights and permissions for work published and unpublished; amend contracts for the benefit of heirs; work out editing and publishing schedules for manuscripts in various stages of completion.'

In retirement Giroux lived quietly with his partner of fifty years, Charles Reilly. He finally published his book on Shakespeare's sonnets, *The Book Known as Q*, generously dedicated to Van Doren and Berryman (Frank Kermode described it in a 1983 *NYRB* piece as the work of 'a well-informed layman'. A 'condescending phrase' Giroux replied in print). He died in 2008. At his memorial service, Pat Strachan, once Giroux's assistant, remembered his stoicism, except: 'In the winter of 1972 Bob called me into his office, asking me to shut the door. After I sat down, he said, "John has jumped off the bridge." Tears began streaming down his face. His beloved John Berryman had taken his own life'.

Poems

Francis O'Hare

Blue

Miles Davis. *Kind of Blue*.
The sound of subways, sidewalks, New

York, in early springtime, dew
gleaming on the traffic queue-

ing over Brooklyn Bridge, the view
of morning filled with such a hue

of sadness it would trouble you
into playing the trumpet too.

Lost Weekends

I've had Lost Weekends.
Lost weekdays too. The fog
of alcohol descends,
the floor becomes a bog
and down I go, *sans* friends,
sans everything, *glug*, *glug*...

I've had dark sojourns
in the shadow-smoky vale
eyeing beers and bourbons
along the supermarket aisle,
their 'Drink Me' in bright neons,
their easy charm, their guile...

I've had Ray Milland
moments, I can tell you,
cracked up moments, and
ended up in Bellevue.
I'd have you understand,
though, that sanity is hell too...

Memento

Picture this:
a young woman,
her back to us,
in sleety rain,

above her, sky
Soviet-grey,
a seagull's cry
not far away,

a cold air which
reminds us of
Shostakovich,
The Second Waltz,

and swirls us back
to Leningrad,
that paranoiac
world frost-clad,

but she is music –
is violins,
is clarinets
and saxophones,

her body light
as a melody,
or a dove in flight
above the sea.

She wears a hood
against the weather
so what her mood
is, we never gather

until she turns
(remember this)
on us. And burns
like ice. Like roses.

Order

John FitzGerald

Whereas love is a four-letter word
without cursive complication,

whereas love can roll over ungloved,
and is cloven and clover-leaved,

whereas love will fester in the
suprasternal notch of the beholden,

whereas love permits lust, and lust
perversion, and perversion pain,

whereas love poses a threat to the
sustainability of the sedulous line,

whereas love disrespects solity,
which is to say is rife, at play, abroad –

I issue the following Emergency Order.

All social contact requires strict use
of appropriate protective syntax.

Palatal implosives must not be voiced
in any language except Swahili.

All citizens must record their dreams
(excess fish will prompt enquiry).

Memories must not be revived,
kicking through leaves, or shelling peas.

Do not look intently at clouds
while uttering weak verbs.

Use of mirrors is prohibited except for
orthodontics and during exorcism.

Accordingly, be it known that

agents have scoured all able etymons
for hate which will tear at the heart of the Earth

from the heat of this moment, repulsing
all pyrophosphates, and chateaubriand,

and obliterating the even more potent
odium to which chatelaines aspire.

With hate here to stay, available,
inherent, whatever,

I order furthermore –

no dad and daughter spoofs,
no weak preterites, no variants in a pair,

no remorse on exit, no more ad executives
coming up with campaigns to forget Pinochet,

no bloody kintsugi, no bad ransomware,
no handy ablatives, no gap analysis,

no high jinks at the ice rink,
no volent jim-hickeys in pullovers

crawling all over our science
to upend this tremendous revolt.

‘Parabolas of love’: Poetry and the Philosophy of Mathematics

ANDREW WYNN OWEN

Great Circles: The Transits of Mathematics and Poetry by Emily Rolfe Grosholz (Springer), €34

Great Circles is remarkable for its compound accomplishment, fusing knowledge of poetry, mathematics, and philosophy, and putting forward persuasive arguments about connections between poetry and mathematics. Some connections refer to shared foundational interests in ontology. Some refer to parts of the subject matter of poetry, and indeed of our general understanding of the world, that are subjects of mathematical investigation (e.g. the infinite, circles, fractals, particularly as they participate in cosmology). The book is also peppered with excerpts from Grosholz's remarkable poetical works. These interludes movingly explore the kinds of feelings (wonder, perplexity, joy, etc.) that the ideas prompt. I will attempt some summary, then add a few thoughts.

Part I, ‘A Life in Mathematics and Poetry’, which includes Chapters 1–4 (‘The House of Childhood’, ‘Music and Hyperspace’, ‘Great Books’, ‘Home, Cambridge, Paris: A Family’), contains moving oscillation between subjective reminiscence and objective knowledge, a juxtaposition that will be of interest again in the book's coda. There is discussion of the use of ambiguity in poetry; how ambiguity can give rise to mathematical discovery; how a sphere can be everted. A section on Ernst Cassirer leads to reflections on myth: ‘Cassirer concludes that philosophy's task is not to eliminate myth but to understand it, locating it within the whole (rich, plural, unstable) system of culture’ (48). Cassirer believed in ‘the objectivity of the artistic imagination’ (45). His work is important for its emphasis on many-sided awareness, ‘Opposing the tendency to elevate a single kind of symbolic form and deny legitimacy to others’: ‘the recognition of incommensurable symbolic forms demands that philosophy engage in a continually renewed effort of reflection’ (48–9). Cassirer viewed Kant as a thinker with a vision of hopefulness in the face of ultimate unfulfilment, positioning humans as driven by a quest for knowledge that can never finally be satisfied. This was opposed, in a debate at Davos, to Heidegger's interpretation, which emphasised a disconcerting ‘abyss beneath the throne of reason’, as David Nirenberg has put it. These are two valid facets of Kantian interpretation: human limitation can lead on to despair about the whole project of reason; or, the Cassirean way, it can lead to a tempered trust in reason. Cassirer is an attractive figure for philosophers who take art seriously, and artists who take philosophy seriously, and, as Grosholz observes, appreciation of his contribution is timely. A rationalist and idealist with respect for art and science, Cassirer will be of particular interest to artists who intuit the goodness of what they do and its connection to important aspects of reality. His appearance in these biographical chapters helps to establish a broad ontological and epistemological background for the book. As Nirenberg notes, Cassirer's ‘lapidary answer’ to the question of what human beings are was that they are, in Cassirer's words, ‘capable of form’ (‘When Philosophy Mattered’, *The New Republic*, 2011).

Part II, ‘The Homestead’, concerns geometry. Chapter 5, ‘What's in a Circle? Spinoza, Leibniz, Marlowe, Shakespeare, Keats’, discusses the history of mathematical interest in the circle, how such interest resurfaces and reorients according to the understanding available at any given time, and relates the cosmological significance of circles to poetical interest. Cosmology serves as a bridge from mathematics to poetry. Poetry's ‘elaborate formal periodicities’ are mentioned. A Spinozist ‘Ode to Butterflies’ (‘Cutouts of God's great fabric—matter—divine confetti // Thrown necessarily up’) reminded this reader that the Greek ψυχή (psyche) is the word for ‘mind’, ‘soul’, and ‘butterfly’ – many cultures have myths relating butterflies to souls, and it is interesting to see them appear in art. One may also be reminded, in this chapter, of the baffling description of God as a sphere whose centre is everywhere and whose circumference is nowhere. The description of mathematical research on circles, evolving to consider new questions in light of the accumulation of knowledge, recalls Seamus Heaney's ‘Wheels Within Wheels’, a poem containing many circles: ‘But enough was not enough. Who ever saw / The limit in the given anyhow?’

Chapter 6 is titled ‘Four Master Tropes, from Euclid to Leibniz, with Burke’. (Those seeking Edmund Burke should look elsewhere: this is the theorist Kenneth Burke.) We learn about some of the limits of Greek mathematical understanding: ‘The boundaries of Greek geometry, I think, may best be indicated in historical retrospect positively by the metaphor of construction and the middle term of the proportion between ratios, and negatively by the absence of true algebraic notation, as a decisive limit and boundary’ (102). The development of algebra, ‘from the tenth to the thirteenth century in the Arabic world’ (107) and then later in Europe, allowed people ‘to think number and figure together’ (110). The chapter closes with the happy image of Leibniz ‘inspired by the clouds over the Harz Mountains, where he served the Court of Hannover as a mining engineer, supervising the draining of the silver mines ... by installing wind machines’ (110). Chapter 7, ‘Periodicity as Symmetry in Time: Housman’, clarifies the proposition that poetry is generally structured by periodicities: ‘Periodicity is symmetry in time’ (115). ‘Natural systems, like molecules, cells, organisms, solar systems, stars and galaxies, exhibit stability that persists for a while, and then disperses. Their stability is manifest in geometric forms that are often highly symmetrical, and that express a "low" energetic state in contrast to other more highly excited, unstable possible states of the same system' (113). This may seem to some merely a good 'way of putting it', to borrow T. S. Eliot's phrase from *Four Quartets*, but it is more than a way of putting it: it is true. Those who have spent many hours putting words in intricate patterned arrangements will probably, from introspection, be moved to endorse Grosholz's view that this enterprise is an expression of our desire to resist the destructive advance of entropy and to commune somehow with abiding structures of reality.

Part III, 'Shipping Out', concerns dynamics. Chapter 8, 'Troping in Italian Gardens: Descartes, Wallis, La Hire, Gassendi', has at its heart a discussion of disagreement between Descartes and Gassendi concerning the mind-body problem. There is fascinating description of how mechanical ideas, such as the 'hydraulic metaphor' (136), were used to explain processes that animate life. The deep proposition of this chapter comes when Grosholz writes, 'In defense of Descartes, I argue that the middle term which brings *res extensa* and *res cogitans* into rational relation, is in fact mathematics'. That is to say, with only a slight shift in terminology: mathematics is the source of the epistemic link between matter and mind. This implies the variety of objective idealism known as 'ideationalism'. Leslie Armour writes, 'There are many sorts of "idealism." Mentalism is one, stoutly and well defended recently by the late, much-lamented Timothy Sprigge. Ideationalism, the thesis that the real consists of what some Platonists (but likely not Plato) called ideas, is another'.(See 'A Conversation with Leslie Armour' by Ian Angus, in *Symposium: Canadian Journal of Continental Philosophy*, p. 77.)

Epistemological concerns also shape Chapter 9, 'Flow, Rest, Inertial Motion: Wilner, Di Piero, Bonnefoy', which draws a distinction between poets who believe time is unreal and those who believe it real: the anti-realists about time are identified with 'Parmenidean (and Spinozist) metaphysics', the realists with 'Heraclitean (and Whiteheadian) metaphysics'. This distinction gives rise to some remarkable, intricate and feeling literary analysis. Along the way, there is ideationalism: describing a poem by Dorothy Roberts, Grosholz summarises, 'Patterns are objective: the mind encounters them; it does not invent them' (149). There is mentalism: 'mind is the stubborn stability in nature' (151). We learn that 'inertial motion confounds, or unites, time and eternity': 'Poets thus often use inertial motion as a figure of thought to evoke the divinity or numinousness of human experience, especially those heightened, intense episodes that so appealed to the Romantics' (156). This leads into a translation of Bonnefoy, the advocate of *présence.*

Chapter 10, 'Troping Towards the Transcendental: Napier, Newton, Leibniz', discusses the emergence of the infinitesimal calculus and its significance: 'The application of Cartesian algebra to "transcendent things" changes algebra itself to produce the "infinitesimal calculus," whose immediate consequence is to generalize and simplify, as well as to offer a deeper-lying explanation of why algebra brings together the study of series of numbers and that of curves so effectively' (173). Integration, leading toward transcendental curves, is more difficult than differentiation: 'The behavior of differential operators can be captured in a closed algebra ... whereas integration eludes such formalization, as its domain eludes closure' (169). Quotation from Leibniz conveys the excitement of mathematical discovery, particularly as it affirmed his staunch rationalism ('Transported by joy at this first theorem' (172)). The discussion of Leibniz connects with the account of the historical development of mathematical knowledge in previous chapters: 'Remember Archimedes making use of it [the curve as infinite-sided polygon], but coming up short? He didn't have algebra yet' (173). The book's explanatory language of synecdoche, metonymy, and middle term recur persuasively.

Part IV, 'The Sky's the Limit!', concerns infinity. Chapter 11, 'Compactifiction: Randall, Fainlight, Sedakova', suggests that poems present a 'tug of war' between 'temporality' ('its successiveness as the reader moves from line to line') and 'spatiality' ('its shape, which becomes a figure for the transcendence of time'). Time is the taking away, the thing that takes loved ones from us and eventually our own lives (at least, it seems so), so it is natural that those who are not deeply despondent should oppose it. 'If a poet is fond of stasis, there are two problems: death and eternity' (198). The chapter focuses on three poets 'who do not love succession': 'They employ repetition in a certain way, and they are especially fond of circles and rings' (181). This is a memorable insight about the meaningfulness of circles for some poets. There is a discussion of mathematical 'compactification', which stops points running off to infinity by putting 'points at infinity'. 'Thus we can set up a one-to-one correspondence between the infinite Euclidean line and the circle, and the infinite Euclidean plane and the sphere' (182). 'Here is another way of putting it, from projective geometry: the line goes off in two different directions, forever; but if we add the point at infinity at either end, and identify infinity with itself, we can consider the line a circle' (183). But before readers go thinking that this might endorse eternal recurrence in reality, it is worth noting that a lot rests on 'identify[ing] infinity with itself' and there is no certain parallel between the mathematical infinite line and the timeline in reality. After a passage from Sedakova, ending in the memorable exhortation 'So go ahead faster or I'll leave you behind', Grosholz presents a persuasive view of the abiding purpose of poetry, its access to 'the heart of things': 'the aim of poetry is to recreate, to go to the heart of things, to find or lament the hidden ring that lies in darkness' (200).

Chapter 12, 'Beyond Deduction: From Descartes to Gödel', discusses the transformation of mathematical understanding of number and figure, and the road that took mathematicians 'to master the infinite' (205). There is a humorous swipe against logicism, the attempt to reduce mathematics to logic: 'a very dangerous infection of the brain, which tends to go viral' (206). (For those unfamiliar: the story of some of this is summarised, for the case of Frege, Russell, and Whitehead, in the entertaining graphic novel *Logicomix: An Epic Search for Truth.*) The mention of 'Spinoza's necessity' (225) is a reminder of the part of Spinozism to which people who are otherwise persuaded may take exception, its denial of free will, a part that Wordsworth jettisoned in *The Prelude*. But it is possible to take many lessons from Spinozism without accepting its rigid determinism. Even Spinoza seems to have been inconsistent in this aspect of his philosophy: as Bennett (1984) writes, 'many textual details plus much of the broad outline of Spinoza's moral theory can be nicely explained on the conjecture that it is a morality not of causal self-sufficiency but rather of completeness of voluntary control ... if in Part 4 he is largely thinking in terms of what is internal or external to the will—as I think he is—this is something for which he has not even the pretence of a foundation earlier in the *Ethics*' (*A Study of Spinoza's Ethics*, p. 328).

Chapter 13, 'Literary Cosmology: Plato, Tobin, Major, Turner', discusses 'one way that mathematics enter directly into poetry': cosmology. We encounter Plato's argument in the *Timaeus* about the limitations of materialism: 'Plato objects that materialism must stop at the second level of the Divided Line ontologically, so its epistemology can never rise above the level of common sense, or worse, of rumor; that is, it can never aspire to science or philosophy' (232). Grosholz summarises: 'materialism grasps a deep though partial metaphysical truth, the necessity of embodiment for recognizing the image as image, for distinguishing image from object, for knowing oneself, for reflectiveness, for the wisdom of mortality' (235). It is interesting, among other things, to learn that 'one of the main challenges to Einstein's presentation of General Relativity came from a physicist who was also a Belgian priest, Georges Lamaître' (238): he proposed that space-time 'was not only curved, but dynamic', which, after a period of denial, Einstein came to accept.

Grosholz's lyric poems are scattered throughout the book and are often presented as reflective spin-offs from the mathematical and philosophical discussion. The prose part of a chapter will typically end, 'So I wrote this poem' (174). The reader feels challenged to fit the ideas in the prose with the first-person experiences conveyed by these pieces. This is an important humanistic task, with much groundwork generously laid by Grosholz herself, because while the kind of knowledge conveyed in this book is mostly characteristic of an objective way of looking at reality, lyric poetry, by contrast, deals in conveying the quality and structure of subjective conscious experience. I am thinking here of Thomas Nagel's distinction, in *Mortal Questions* (1973), between the objective and subjective ways of looking at the world. Nagel writes that bearing subjectivity in mind is 'particularly important in connexion with philosophical problems about free will, personal identity, agent-centered morality, or mind and body, which cannot be dealt with in detachment from the subjective point of view on which they depend for their existence'. Lyric poetry is an art form that can reveal at least some of the value and contents of subjectivity to the mind. It is therefore a bulwark against the sceptical partiality and moral despondency that may derive from ignoring subjective considerations. The problems Nagel mentions are not the philosophical problems at the heart of this book, but they are felt strongly in the wings by means of the poetry. Thus, aside from participation in debates about the philosophy of mathematics, Grosholz's book also engages in a truly unusual way in another difficult debate, namely that between objective and subjective ways of understanding the world. Nagel anticipates the artistic mediation of debates of this kind: 'The task of accepting the polarity [between subjectivity and objectivity] without allowing either of its terms to swallow the other should be a creative one'. In this vein, Grosholz provides many precise and evocative phrases that seek to bridge the divide: 'the frail parabolas of love' (104), 'flanks / Of the tangent mountains' (138), 'The tears in things dissolve geometry' (139). The mind-body note recurs and is often very moving: 'Thus rivers freely flow / According to the principle of least work, / That, like the *Odes* of Pindar, gently governs / Spirit wound in matter's labyrinth.' (228). Grosholz is clear-eyed about human limitation but far more content, in well-informed and optimistic Cassirean fashion, about knowledge and its limits than, for example, W. B. Yeats (who wrote, of his soul, 'fastened to a dying animal / It knows not what it is'). One villanelle presents a refrain-line 'We can't remember half of what we know' and the halved unreliability of the memory of knowledge is then reflected in the silver-gold pairing of 'life' and 'decay' in the final stanza: 'The silver trees spring back to life, although / Their roots are gilded by the leaves' decay' (116). The implication is that, as biological existence is divided between growth and decline, so knowledge has its joyful affordances and grave silences.

A 'Coda' puts forward an interesting 'series of terms' that serves as a spectrum, presenting 'Concept' and 'Myth' at one end, and 'Person' and 'Life' at the other. This is reminiscent of Philip Sidney's distinction between philosophy and history, the rationalist discipline and the empiricist one: 'The philosopher therefore and the historian are they which would win the goal, the one by precept, the other by example; but both not having both, do both halt' ('The Defense of Poesy'). Grosholz makes the point that 'there is no "pure experiential agent" hovering on the right side of the diagrammatic array ... Nor is there anything hovering on the left side: pure concepts do not enter into moral or poetic or mathematical discourse, unconnected to stories' (257). F. H. Bradley would have disagreed that 'there is no "pure experiential agent"', believing in the reality of 'centres of experience' and the illusoriness of the self. Grosholz's implied answer to those who speak against the reality of the self is supported by analogy between literature and life. She continues with a discussion of Prospero and *The Tempest*: 'we see that in one and the same play, some characters live near the historical edge of the spectrum I just offered, and some live near the conceptual edge' (257). The book ends with the presence of Bonnefoy, the author of *Anti-Platon* (1947), who wrote, 'marcherons-nous sur les ruines d'un ciel immense', and who sits complicatedly near Prospero's declaration: 'my ending is despair, / Unless I be relieved by prayer'.

Let us now consider what kind of literary criticism this book might prompt, when its lessons are synthesised. I will take as test case the work of a brilliantly skilful and compassionate poet, Gwendolyn Brooks. The following extract is from 'The Children of the Poor', a series of deeply moving Petrarchan sonnets:

And shall I prime my children, pray, to pray?
Mites, come invade most frugal vestibules
Spectered with crusts of penitents' renewals
And all hysterics arrogant for a day.
Instruct yourselves here is no devil to pay.
Children, confine your lights in jellied rules;
Resemble graves; be metaphysical mules.
Learn Lord will not distort nor leave the fray.

The tragedy of the poem is permeated by the thoughts implied by its mathematical structure. The putting of words in patterns governed by mathematical rules, and the resultant intensity of emotional and artistic effect, which would not have been conveyed to anything like the same degree by the same thoughts expressed in prose, gives rise to an intuition about the generalisability of our ideas about objectivity. 'If numbers can operate through language to produce highly emotional and artistic effects,' the thought goes, 'then it seems more probable that the discipline of mathematics describes a very deep kind of truth, perhaps an objective truth, existing independent of our minds.' This is the intuition of the mathematical Platonist, and it can be fanned by all sorts of other things. 'And I suppose,' the thought continues, 'that the other thing the poem is clearly deeply interested in might also be objective: morality.' This is the intuition of the moral realist, and it can also be fanned by all sorts of other things. The poem synthesises mathematical Platonism and moral realism. This is a high achievement, yoking two important aspects of reality. Consider Rowan Williams's answer, when asked, 'What is God?': 'a synthesis of love and mathematics'. And it is worth noting here that such a remark, though certainly gesturing towards something vast and extraordinary, is limited when compared to F. H. Bradley's vision of reality, which saw a truly all-encompassing substance monism: 'Nothing is lost to the Absolute, and all appearances have reality' (*Appearance and Reality* (1893), p. 495). Love (understood here, selectively, as another way of saying 'morality') and mathematics are aspects of mind, but they do not have the explanatory reach of a mindlike substance (whether it be called mind, or spirit, or experience). This is where the mentalism of some idealists goes further, as an explanatory presupposition about reality, than the ideationalism of the Platonists.

Nicolai Hartmann thought there were 'at least two main types of ideal entities, namely mathematical entities and values', and this led him to interesting considerations: 'the question arises: what else, apart from atemporality, is shared by the entities included in the sphere of ideal being' (*Stanford Encyclopedia*). Hartmann identified three general features shared by the two types of ideal entities: overall unknownness to us; extension 'beyond the boundaries of real being'; both 'claim universality' but neither are 'able to capture—from their own point of view—the whole of reality' (*Stanford Encyclopedia*). Brooks's poem suggests that there is an objective aspect to reality, a moral reality, which stands independent of human thought, and speaks against those who do wrong. The poem is also structured in such a way that it suggests that there is another objective aspect, the mathematical, which somehow coexists with this. It is therefore a vessel for two deep views about reality. There is also some relation between these views implied by its artistic unity. All of Hartmann's three shared features can be felt when reading Brooks's poem: there is anguished wonder at unknownness; there is apprehension of the possibility of realms extending beyond 'real being'; there is a perplexed sense of the incompleteness of both mathematics and morality for describing all of reality. Grosholz's book is concerned with the two ideal realms, those of mathematics and values, and the kinds of art on which she focuses also often draw inspiration from these. A poetry that seeks to explore the connections between these realms would spend time considering the three areas outlined by Hartmann. (Hartmann also comes to mind when reading *Great Circles* for another reason: Cassirer, epistemological opponent of Heidegger, is valorised; Hartmann presents the major alternative to Heidegger's view in ontology.)

But the kind of analysis I have done here so far is very general and could be applied to many moving poems in pattern. I will attempt a more specific kind of comment, and thereby hope to show that the Grosholzian critical avenue might give rise to the sort of potential for variety that broad critical methodologies require. Here it is worth considering the lines: 'Children, confine your lights in jellied rules; / Resemble graves; be metaphysical mules'. It does not sound good to 'Resemble graves' or be 'metaphysical mules'. Mules are known for carrying things and being stubborn. It may well be interpreted as bitterly stating horror at the kind of quietist outlook that, some believe, deadens people while alive ('Resemble graves'). But there is sharp and fascinating ambiguity here: 'metaphysical mules' are fitting things to be sometimes, even in grievously difficult situations, for personal resilience. The universe sends tragedy and mystery our way, and our freedom is sometimes limited to bearing it stubbornly, while doing what we can to know and pursue the good. The phrase 'metaphysical mules' is remarkable because it speaks both for and against the weight that it bears. 'And shall I prime my children, pray, to pray?' is a vast question, speaking, as the best poetry does, with sincerity both to its terrible circumstances and to all time (at least, all times in which there are conscious beings who reproduce). It would be glib, given the depth of suffering and unknownness in the universe for limited beings like us, to answer with a simple yes or no.

This is not Practical Criticism: it has clearer 'metaphysical grounding' than Practical Criticism usually has and is generally understood as having. But it is clearly not pure theory, so not Theoretical Criticism either. It is that difficult thing, then, praised by Coleridge: a compound criticism, a Practical-Theoretical Criticism, one that hopefully begins to take account of the deep tragic joy that poetry often points toward. The normal critical practice of parsing ambiguity and permuting semantic intricacies can operate more effectively and directedly within the metaphysical framework. It is in this way that students of literature can achieve a double focus on what Grosholz calls 'the thicket of the particular' and 'the great arch of the universal' (149). And it is in this way, perhaps, that poets may maintain their position as valuable interpreters of reality.

The Third Wish

Maurice Riordan

My last was the Soul's last draught – the taste almost
  remembered – of the Body's elixir.
And so it is – it's blind chance – I'm outside the canted
  walk-up block on Main St West braced
and maybe kept in place by, on the roof, a giant
  billboard telling me this blue morning
I've *come to where the flavor is.* Marlboro Country.
  Not a soul in sight. Signs everywhere.
A Sprite on the table gone flat, on the turntable Blondie's
  Call Me. Bathwater scuzzy. Cold.
And now in the air shaft *Arum dem fayer* – next door's
  pure contralto while she showers.
I break open a Molson X, slide on *Nighthawks*,
  twirl the channels... hockey, the seal hunt,
Carter's twitching face, an angry blackclad chorus – kid
  on a metal leg running in a blizzard
          Shoyn genug
In bafflement and loneliness I betake my lithe,
  my featherlite Mark Spitz new bod,
East to Hanrahan's and fall in with Bob Kennedy
  theonetheydidntshoot on Shuffleboard.
We take on the bleary night shift in from Stelco.
  Truckers off the 403. Skinning them,
Bob pocketing our bets to buy Su and Gipsy
  – over for the week from Buffalo –
shots between their sets. *And donate the Cancer Kid.*
  Dude with steel peg on that fool run.
Cross the whole goddammit country! I hop it to the can,
  donate my last quarter to the payphone
only to hear it ring out once more.
          Thunder
  as I unfurl into *what a night*. Jog
along Barton in a downpour, the Expressway
  a glazed arcade I ghost across to locate
the mudtrack through Cootes Paradise, and home past
  the dismantled elms, the Bowling Green,
where a moonstruck she-chuck's brought her kits
  where a month ago or one before
we made angels. I stop for a puff beside the Shul
  but ma chuck's wise to my perfume.
I give her the Jesus sign and slip away. Sneak a leak
  back of Mike's Submarines, then hit
the hay as swollen-fingered dawn ignites a bonfire
  under the Lake. And fall in a swound.

  Hello (a seamless join) she's softly in
the door frame, all smiles. All planned it seems. *Weekend*
  out West with Bunny and with Mum.
A clutch under her oxter of dog-eared term papers.
  But the noon sky above Marlboro Country's
skyblue and we scarper diem up the escarpment,

bumping bikes along beside the railroad,
she in cut-off jeans and cotton top – where a sweat map
unfolds as we lean into the climb.
And a Canadian Pacific's pulls past us uphill slow
heading for the heartlands – we hoick
the bikes on to an empty flatcar. Lifts us over the brow.

Should we have stayed aboard? Bound
for the Sault and Thunder Bay, found a door to other lives
or vanished in the boreal sublime...?
Thing is you haven't a clue. You're in the thick of moods.
Swings. The grip of some MacGuffin.
And every ego-punch and knockdown, each rare sweet trade,
all the aggregate of being true or kind,
is not a blank (since nothing in the end surprises us).
The face on the pillow. Our kids' twin-flame.
Those suited folk on the concourse who wave and smile.
One who seems to look into the soul.
Even the half-heard newsflash fits some jigsaw dream.
But we're untuned. There's noise. No frame.
What to make of these muscle-bound cars along the street?
While the Scotty or Jean-Luc zipping by
isn't jet-propelled but on a Schwinn! While the same mustard
school bus stands next the Mission Church.

We lower the bikes on to fireweed and break into woods
above Dundas. Pick out the Indian trail.
Blue jays scuffle in the brush. Blades of light dazzle
the treetops... a rose-breast grosbeak in flight?
While woodpeckers camouflaged in chequered shade hammer out
some half-remembered code... but it fades.
The grove is hushed and we push on through pine litter
in rustling silence, then watch ourselves
emerge. Revenants behind the new developments.
From where it's downhill back to Mike's.
Me now on good old mudguardless brakeless 'baldie'
(I got it for a song one Harvest Fayre),
my sneakers sparking off asphalt as we round each bend.
There's burn each side of the back strap
and beads of – mercury, honeydew? – across her spine.
Or rivulets of rain... run-stop sideways
retrieved from an InterCity window outside Leeds.

It's *Smokey's* last day at The Westdale,
a line backed up the sidewalk to Piccone's ice cream.
Dust devils shimmy in the car lot.
We sprint for the screen door, take the stairs' rungs three
at a time, a foot race to the icebox,
a dead heat to our little room – the bed let's not forget
pledged to Chris the basement medic,
Christophe and Marta, or Maria, his Coptic bride,
tapping her bump the very day the Kid
pulls out of his run (losing a fight he's also won)
and storms break from Huron to the Gulf.
Chris-smiling-signing-Marta make angels on our bed.
They like its royal fit. We nudge them
to its purchase, then give it them for free. For love.
The island place we rowed to in our dream.
Whence through an eyelet of the night I'm whisked away.

Reviews

Piece by Piece

Scattered Limbs, **Iain Bamforth**
(Galileo Publishers) £16.99
Reviewed by Kirsty Gunn

There are so many things going on in an essay. There's the pleasure of impress, for a start, upon the mind. That sense upon reading of gaining immediately relation to the text; nothing here is to be won or strained after or even missed.

Then there's the personal aspect of the thing. Of being in the company of someone who has made thinking and writing part of their life's work and who wants to engage the reader in that process. We shall go through this together, the essay says. I have no idea much where I am headed, but how agreeable it is that you are here with me for the journey. So is the essay movement, talk. It is not the result of prior thoughts and summaries, someone catching you in their grip and jawing on. It has never, heaven forbid, a drum to beat, or a march to call. Nor is it 'about' an idea; instead it becomes one. The essay really is intimate – 'The voice in your ear of someone you rather like', as one of America's foremost essayists and a great champion for the form, Phillip Lopate, put it, at a conference about essays held in Arbroath (Taking Ideas for a Walk: A conference on the Essay held at Hospitalfied House, Arbroath) a year or so ago.

How civilised the form, then. Not hustling to be entertainment or wanting to grab the limelight with one big idea. Essays want to muse and digress, and Iain Bamforth muses and digresses most gloriously in *Scattered Limbs*, a collection of parts that come together in one body of breathing, living thinking. Here are essays readers of this magazine will recognise from the author's 'Catchwords' column – for their fragmentary style, their wry diffidence, a casual laying down of one idea here, often no more than a paragraph, and another there, perhaps a bit longer, to take its place below. Iain Bamforth is a poet as well as a medical doctor, a reader of myth as well as anatomies – and this sensibility, of one who easily arranges a piece about science along with one on imagination, means the accumulation of his thought arrives with us much as a set of poems might, with gaps of white space between to account for the exquisite depth charges which have gone off in each as happily as fireworks. Yet how they have changed the landscape even so. Here he is, in 'Emotion Studies', leaping from 'Emotions are elaborate kinds of disclosures and beckonings' that can never be fixed, 'ethical ways of apprehending the world, and yet we are largely clueless about them' to, in 'More Body Parts' on the facing page, 'Why do we utter "My Foot!" as a dismissive ejaculation?' After all, he writes, the French say '*mon oeil!*', and '*Tu prends ton pied?*' means to ask whether ejaculation, in another sense, has indeed occurred. In a couple of paragraphs we've been jolted from one kind of feeling to another, setting the concept of a self and its odd language into a merry spin.

The slight appearance of these essays is gorgeous. Voice in the ear indeed! Allowing a whisper of a thought, a shy, sly presentation of a fact to lead on to some other connection that then quite easily changes the way we think about a thing, or deepens it... That is Iain Bamforth's great technique. *Techne,* he reminds us modestly in 'Crafts', was not something the gods were ever going to come down on hard. If we showed ourselves as tip-top at, say, lyre playing or pottery, there would be no call for hubris, only the reward which comes from doing a thing and doing it pretty fabulously. 'It was only after... the First World War, when the machine seemed to have won, that the word "craft" became derisory – a past time for eccentrics and the slightly loopy.'

Well, *Scattered Limbs* may not augur wrath from Olympus, only my feeling is that there's more than expertise on show here, in this glorious collection. The subtitle of *Scattered Limbs* is *A Medical Dreambook* and while it is indeed an 'incubator' of phantoms, as Iain Bamforth describes his project, surreal and groping thoughts coming at us from all directions out of the dark, this is surely logopoeia we are witnessing. One finishes reading not as though from breaking sleep, but out of a sense of having had time out in a state of vivid consciousness. What's more, we awake with a smile on our faces and a feeling of, yes, great joy.

The Age of Phillis

***The Age of Phillis*, Honorée Fanonne Jeffers (Wesleyan UP) £19.95**
Reviewed by Andrew Hadfield

There are few more important enigmas in the history of English poetry than Phillis Wheatley. The first African-American author of a book of poetry, Phillis Wheatley (1753–84) was the name given to her by the slave-owning couple who bought her, John and Susannah Wheatley. The real name of the poet, who was probably born in Gambia or Senegal, is not known. She arrived in Boston in 1761 when she was about eight, on the slave ship, *Phillis*, which the Wheatleys used to provide her slave name. Accordingly, convention now is to refer to her as Phillis Wheatley Peters, her married name, as that was one of the few choices she was able to make in her life in colonial America (and a married name has at least as much dignity as that of a ship).

Wheatley Peters was a precocious talent: under the Wheatleys' tutelage she learned Latin and Greek and started to write poetry as a teenager. She travelled to London in 1773 and her volume, *Poems on Various Subjects, Religious and Moral*, was published later that year. The Wheatleys emancipated her and she married John Peters, a free black grocer. According to some testimony (not necessarily reliable) the couple had three children, all of whom died young, and descended into poverty, either the result of John's improvidence (like Ann Hathaway, John Peters is frequently blamed without reliable evidence, for the unhappiness of his brilliant spouse) or, more plausibly, the economic effects of the Revolutionary War through which the couple lived. Phillis, never a healthy young woman, died at the age of thirty-one, probably about as many years as she could expect, perhaps while her husband was in prison.

Wheatley Peters spent the first quarter of her life in West Africa so must have been able to remember significant details of her childhood. However, her poems retain no traces of her early years and she is known for the loyalty and gratitude she expresses for her good fortune and the advantages offered by colonial society, most famously in her dense short lyric, 'On Being Brought From Africa to America':

> 'Twas mercy brought me from
> my *Pagan* land,
> Taught my benighted soul to
> understand
> That there's a God, that there's
> a *Saviour* too:
> Once I redemption neither
> sought nor knew.
> Some view our sable race with
> scornful eye,
> 'Their colour is a diabolic die.'
> Remember, *Christians*, *Negros*,
> black as *Cain*,
> May be refin'd, and join th'
> angelic train.

It's a neat and forceful poem, centred around an obvious poetic conceit, the contrast between the two extremes of light and dark, and there is a stern reminder for backsliding, racist white Christians, that black people can be just as virtuous believers as they are. It is not a message that modern readers are likely to find palatable, and the question is whether Wheatley Peters did herself. Was she so enmeshed in American society that she could dismiss the land of her parents and ancestors as pagan, rejoicing at her enforced deracination, and seeing the colour of her own skin as something to be overcome, refined and effectively washed white? The activist and poet, Amiri Baraka (1934–2014), saw her as a 'race traitor', but she was defended by the powerful voice of Henry Louis Gates Jr, who pointed out the irony that Thomas Jefferson was able to dismiss Wheatley Peters's literature, but was lauded as a liberator of slaves while the enslaved black female poet was regarded as something of an 'Uncle Tom' figure.

The distinguished poet, Honorée Fanonne Jeffers, is clear that Wheatley Peters was a cunning and subversive writer, clever enough to play the games that the authorities demanded but always able to code her messages carefully, speak between the lines, and assert her own identity through her tricksy verbal brilliance. The volume under review here is a mixture of a series of original poems, some written in response to Wheatley Peters's own works; some based on subjects related to her life and experiences and those of other Africans who were forced to cross to America by the Middle Passage; and some written in response to later works from the tradition of black American writing that Wheatley Peters did so much to establish; and a scholarly memoir appended to the poems that outlines the genesis of the collection and the problems facing those wishing to uncover the truth of Wheatley Peters's life. There is also a helpful series of notes for the poems.

Jeffers is certain that Wheatley Peters's consciousness was formed in Africa and that she carried the remnants of her identity – probably Muslim and from the Wolof people – to New England. What connects these poems in the first book, 'Before', is the impossibility of recalling what needs to be remembered and the consequent expunging of identity, as the contemporary poet reflects on her history and her relationship to her mother, a pointed contrast to that of Wheatley Peters:

> A pearl she lives by the sea.
> The strand of a gathered
> Plait. Needed point: surely, love
> doesn't rest in emptied air
> Without some disappointment,

but this is a good moment.
Isn't it? – I can run to my own
playground, remember a cupped
palm next to my ear. I can tell
my mother who is yet alive.

I can claim my memories.
She can answer her ringing
telephone. I won't forget her name
or mine. ('Before the Taking of
Goonay' (child)).

Jeffers herself is conscious that the lives of her ancestors were dislocated and they were forcibly displaced, but they have a tradition that has its roots in another continent, whereas Wheatley Peters had none (the memoir acknowledges that, although her parents taught her to revere Wheatley Peters, they had little time for her poetry). The next poem, 'Fracture', with its insistent, repetitive beat expressing the foreboding of the imminent Atlantic crossing, also charts the erasure of names, here through the breaking up of families and local groups:

The men arrive. The door opens.
The men arrive. The water
welcomes.
The men arrive. The mourning
longs.
The men arrive. Our names shall
scatter.

The moving poem 'Enreaty: Yaay' juxtaposes the bald description of John Wheatley praising her accomplishments and ability to learn at such rapid speed with the anguish of her mother pleading for her return ('still my child / mine / and don't forget me / or this piece of land / oh come back'). In the book, 'After', Susannah Wheatley assumes the role of parent, but things are never going to be quite the same, 'The fickle air between them almost love' ('Mothering 2'). Almost, but not quite. Jeffers wonders whether it was John or Susannah who bought the little slave girl and that she would surely have grasped the nature of the dramatic change in her circumstances, her earlier understanding carried over to the New World: 'Too wise when she tasted / the last of verdancy – / understanding that she was naked, / that heroes strip leaves from the trees / they own?' ('Fathering 2').

The poems work best, I think, when they express an awareness of fissures, gaps that cannot be closed, whatever the desires and assumptions of the protagonists. Caring for her adopted slave when she suffers from asthma, Susannah might have promised 'the waft / of that grieving mother's spirit / that she would keep this daughter safe / yet *enslaved*' ('Susannah Wheatley Tends to Phillis in her Asthmatic Suffering'). Among the most imaginatively successful poems are the lost letters, which quote the words of real or imagined 'originals' interspersed with a disguised voice – or cancelled thoughts – articulating the suppressed truth. A number of these poems involve Samson Occom (1723–92), the native American pastor who was a friend of the Wheatley family. When his mentor, Eleazor Wheelock, redirects funds that Occom helped raise for Moor's Indian Charity School to found instead an elite institution for white boys, the Ivy League Dartmouth College, Occom writes to Susannah Wheatley ostensibly expressing his thanks and affirming his pious faith. However, the text in italics reveals his true feelings:

*(my people scold me for believing
wheelock's lies
that white man who promised to
start a school*

*for the children of my kind he
promised
rooms bordered by brick and wood
that he would teach them tricks of
english*

*that man's a colorless devil like the
one
who spoke scripture in the
wilderness)*
('Lost Letter 4: Samson Occum,
Mohegan, To Susannah
Wheatley, Boston).

The subtext is surely Wheatley's own poem cited above expressing her apparent good fortune in being transported to America and escape from her black, pagan heritage. Native Americans and African slaves alike had learned to imitate the language of the colonial oppressor.

As Jeffers's thoughtful essay on the inspiration for the volume reveals, she is very keen to rehabilitate John Peters from the racist perception of him as a fickle and irresponsible black man incapable of organising his affairs and running a successful business, as well as looking after his wife and family properly. It is an impassioned and reasoned case that leads to the book, 'Love', in which the two free black Americans fall for each other. Wheatley Peters has dreams of the handsome John seeing him as a 'cane-sweet / man who could not break apart, / that John had pretty white teeth' ('Free Negro Courtship 1'). The irony is writ large and small here. It was, of course, sugar cane that brought them to America and made their courtship possible, as cheap labour was needed to grow and harvest the sugar crop and its success would not have been possible without the Atlantic slave trade. John's teeth are attractive but they may be rotted like the sugar they resemble, just as John and Phillis are brought together and destroyed by global forces too powerful for them to understand or resist. 'Lost Letter 19' has Wheatley Peters speaking almost entirely between the lines, the written words, 'I pray you are safe and thriving in Boston, / and I remain your fellow servant in Christ', preceded by her fears for her beloved in the Revolutionary War:

*i had no one else please do not scold
me
if you are waiting for me all will be
well
my love my love my love my love my
love*

Later, in the book 'Liberty', there is a mildly bawdy wedding hymn, acknowledging that now they are free and together they do not have to be restrained by the rules of politeness, respect and gratitude that have determined the nature of their lives. The couple 'walk home / from church, naughty / and able'. They will 'descend to the bed – / *again* – / for the fiftieth or hundredth time.' In the final line Jeffers, aware that she is writing against the grain in defending John Peters, asks the reader to 'Give them this'.

'Revolution' is also among the more striking of the gatherings of poems. It opens with a link between the time of the Declaration of Independence and the advent of the 'Black Lives

Matter' movement, angry at white appropriation of black suffering then and now:

> Redcoats with sneers, in tracts call
> themselves *slaves.*
> Insist they're tethered, yet the
> Africans –
>
> the many souls, the wretched, the
> taken
> who move from *human* to
> *trafficked* –
>
> are ignored as white men don
> paper chains,
> the language of wounded
> throats, chatteled claims.

There is a nice, sly poem addressed to General George Washington – with whom Wheatley Peters did correspond – that cites the original verse letter to the great man (and slave owner) with words in italics crossed out as the real thoughts of the once enslaved poet are carefully hidden. She states that she has taken the freedom to address Washington, '*who I have heard behaves like / either a gentleman or a tyrant / depending on his moods or his money*', the privilege of the entitled. Washington, who appropriates his slave's teeth in his famous wooden dentures, is given a moment of revelation: 'Her quill and life defy my age's Reason. / She steps in God's house, a different season' ('General George Washington Rereads a Poem and Letter he Received from Phillis Wheatley and Agonizes over his Response'). The powerful heroic couplet reads like one of Wheatley Peters's own poems, a sign that her bold logic was getting through to those who mattered, as well as suggesting that a literary dialogue was possible if only (white) people would listen.

The collection ends on a sad note, John Peters addresses his wife from prison just before her death (in the essay/memoir, 'Looking for Miss Phillis', Jeffers explains why she thinks John was in prison when his wife died). Christmas is coming and 'snow will drift through these bars', so he asks her to send him a poem to cheer him up, but there were none left.

The Age of Phillis is a distinguished, interesting and challenging work, based on extensive research and thinking. There are places in which the justified anger of the writer shines through perhaps a little too much. But this is a fitting tribute to a major literary pioneer who should be on every reading list, as well as the work of a mature and confident poet who knows why her work matters too and who can produce lines as pellucid and moving as Phillis Wheatley Peters herself.

'Something is against us'

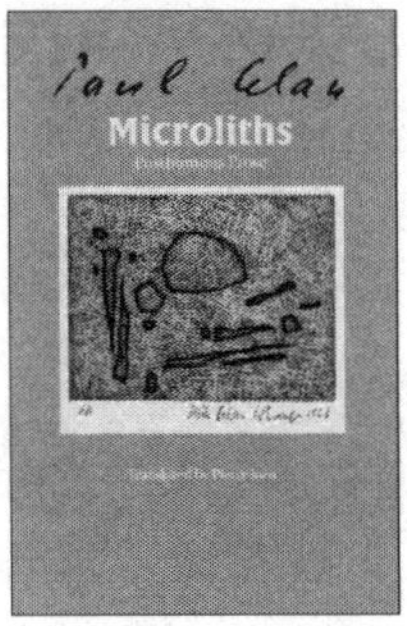

Microliths They Are, Little Stones: Posthumous Prose, **Paul Celan, translated by Pierre Joris (Contra Mundum) £20**
Reviewed by Anthony Barnett

Pierre Joris's translation of Paul Celan's posthumous prose compliments Rosmarie Waldrop's translation of Celan's *Collected Prose* (Carcanet). 'Conversation in the Mountains' therein first appeared in the letterpress pamphlet *The Literary Supplement: Writings*, alongside 'Answer to a Letter' by Edmond Jabès, and a reprint of J. H. Prynne's Celan memorial poem 'Es lebe der König'.

Microliths represents the culmination of Joris's fifty years work on Celan, including two volumes of *Collected Poems* (FSG) and an extraordinary feat in translating drafts and materials for the speech *The Meridian* (Stanford UP). *Microliths* reminds me of George Oppen's *Daybooks* (not a name given them by Oppen), posthumously published piecemeal. Not that Celan's, much shorter in extent, posthumous prose is piecemeal. It is, however, pieces. One may wonder how much of it Celan, as with Oppen, would have been pleased to see in print. That said, there are wonderful aphorisms, narrative prose, notes for dramatic pieces, and mixed blessings among theoretical prose.

The section, 'Texts on the Goll Affair', is devoted to the abuse Celan suffered at the hands of Claire Goll, widow of Ivan Goll, with manufactured charges of plagiarism. Celan helped the Golls in Ivan's dying days, in personal and literary ways. He could not shake off the betrayal. The case is made for this being the catalyst leading to Celan's last mental deterioration and suicide. Celan grapples with his Jewishness: 'something is against us'.

Celan was not always fortunate in the company he kept. That seems to have been more critical for him than the wonderful friends he did have, Nelly Sachs, Ingeborg Bachmann, for example. Fellow Romanian E. M. Cioran crops up. We may never understand why Celan was friendly with a man who upheld the regime that killed his parents, however much Cioran may have sought to repudiate his former self. Then there is Édouard Roditi, who Joris tells us told him Celan was a minor poet. It takes one to know one, or not, for Roditi is the only minor character here. As I wrote elsewhere, in reviewing Franco-Romanian poet Benjamin Fondane, much of what Cioran said in a 1985 conversation leaves a bad taste in the mouth: he rightfully discredits Roditi's wholly deplorable utterances about Celan – in 'Paul Celan and the Cult of Personality' (*World Literature Today*, vol. 66, no. 1, winter 1992) – but he is prone to deplorables himself: 'We were friends. He [Celan] translated one of my books. But we ceased to be friends when he moved to the 16th. That is for me another world—the haute bourgeoisie, and so on, live there: Celan too, since his wife was a marquise. It was finished. In Paris, friendships are a question of neighbourhood'. As far as I know, from my having known Gisèle Celan-Lestrange and Edmond Jabès, that was no bar to the friendship between Celan and Jabès.

It is a task of mine to call publishers to task. The setting of *Microliths* is mostly very readable. But, it is set in Warnock, from Adobe's chief type designer Robert Slimbach. It is he who has foisted on the world the now ubiquitous ghastly crabbed Th ligature (*PNR*'s type is free of it). Contra Mundum also uses overly ornate, as is the italic, ct, sp, st, etc ligatures. They are a distraction. Worse: their books are print-on-demand. I would say nothing about that regrettable way of the world but for the fact that there are two presumptuous, boastful pages of publisher demands for support. They are vulgar. They have no place in *Microliths*.

Pierre Joris is a considerate translator. He weighs every word as far as he finds possible according to the original. His translations of the poems build on pioneering work by Michael Hamburger and John Felstiner in particular. It is hard to see who might follow Joris, though doubtless there will be efforts.

Celan in 'The Conference Project' in *Microliths*: 'I do not speak of the "modern" poem. I speak of the poem today. And to the essential aspects of this today—my today, for I do speak on my own behalf—belongs its lack of a future: I cannot keep from you that I do not know how to answer the question toward which morrow the poem is moving; if the poem borders on such a morrow, then it possesses darkness. The poem's hour of birth, ladies and gentlemen, lies in darkness. Some claim to know that it is the darkness just before dawn; I do not share this assumption.'

Adieu

The Red Scarf: Followed by Two Stages and Additional Notes, **Yves Bonnefoy, translated by Stephen Romer (Seagull Books) £18.99 (hardback)**
Reviewed by Chris Miller

Bonnefoy's last piece of extended prose is a sort of memoir, an exploration of his parents' origins and relationship. But that suggests a book much simpler than this one. For Bonnefoy writes here as the frustrated author of a poetic narrative that would neither resolve itself nor leave him alone. The structure of the book is seemingly determined by Bonnefoy's psychoanalysis of that story; the 'events' of the eponymous poem open out to reveal a suppressed autobiography. We are thus firmly conducted through his own childhood by the interpretative psychopomp.

Barthes, in the non-memoir of his mother, *La Chambre Claire,* bitterly interrogates the hermeneutics of suspicion for a space of innocence in which he can declare his filial love. By contrast, Freud is here the conventional but pliable authority that Bonnefoy brings to bear on his recalcitrant creation. His decision to approach a memoir through his aporetic poem might itself be a defence mechanism, allowing him to see the life of his parents only through the prestige of authorship and the symbols of poetry. Yet our sense of the poet following *l'écharpe rouge* through the labyrinth is convincing and often moving, as each repressive bulkhead dissolves into a further chamber.

'The Red Scarf' of the title is at once the fertility offered by the young wife to the suitor and the consanguinity of the nuclear family. Central to this story is Bonnefoy's guilt; he could not release his father from a silence born of Élie's sense of inadequacy to the intellectual slant of his wife's family, a sense exacerbated by his son's choice of the literary word. Here we might almost be in the English post-Second World War memoir of class betrayal through education. But in 'The Red Scarf', as in the pieces that preceded it and accompany it here, 'Two Scenes' and 'Additional Notes', we are more often in the world of *présence* and Surrealist intuition than of sociology; the central poetic narrative and the 'Two Scenes' are both close to 'automatic' writing. (Bonnefoy's notion of character formed by landscape seems to belong rather to Taine than to Freud.)

The book thus becomes, after that masterpiece *L'Arrière-Pays,* which Romer has also translated, a second volume of poetical autobiography and shares material with the informal sonnets in *Raturer Outre.* Bonnefoy was writing in his nineties, and comparison with *L'Arrière-Pays* can be damaging; he has so often been able, through sentences periodic and circumstantial, to surprise the reader with wonderful conclusions, and, though he still does so, the cost is now higher; his war on the concept as the enemy of the epiphanic and the real alike has moments of dogged insistence, his more elevated rhetoric sometimes drifts free of the argument, and his prose can be clotted. Through this polychrome skein, Romer's translation charts a well-judged course, sometimes enhancing the clarity of his text, at all times imparting rhythmical authority to the English. Bonnefoy chose his translator well. Compliments to Seagull Books on this beautiful edition.

Where eyes are supposed to be

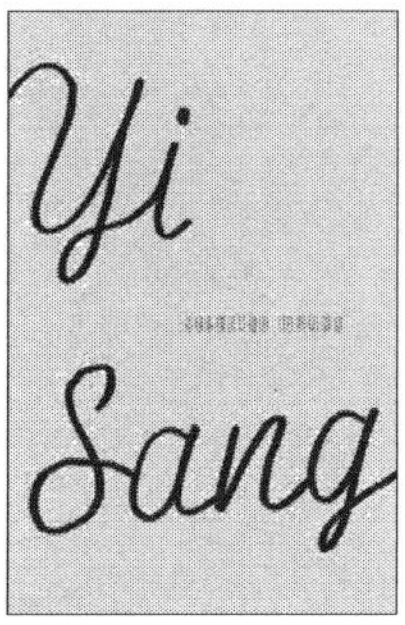

Selected Works, **Yi Sang, edited by Don Mee Choi, translated by Jack Jung, Sawako Nakayasu, Don Mee Choi, and Joyelle McSweeney (Wave Books) $25**
Reviewed by Greg Thomas

The timeline at the start of this selected edition of Yi Sang's (1910–37) work recounts the twin events that set in course his emotional and intellectual development. On 29 August 1910, a month before his birth in Seoul, the Japan-Korea Annexation Treaty was signed, making Korea a formal protectorate of the Japanese Empire. Around four years later, the group of artists and poets who would become known as the Dada movement began to congregate in Zürich.

The works collected in this volume – poems in Korean and Japanese, along with essays and stories – react to the condition of colonial subjugation in a voice of variously displaced rage and trauma, filtered through the anti-rational programmes of Dada and Surrealism. Yi Sang's tone is by turns satirical, morbid, anguished, and brilliantly lurid.

His poems in Japanese – a language brutally enforced upon the annexed Korean state – date mainly from 1931 and seem to take as their animus a desire to dismantle the master's tools and the logical systems encoded therein. Formally elliptical, thematically absurd, one obvious point of reference is Surrealist automatic writing, as in the *slap-in-the-face* gobbets of nonsense which make up 'Beard':

> (BEARD • BEARD • ALL THOSE THINGS • THAT QUALIFY AS FACIAL hair)
> 1
> THERE IS AND WAS A LAUGHTER THAT WAS A FOREST IN THE PLACE WHERE EYES ARE SUPPOSED TO BE
>
> 2
> CARROT

Sawako Nakayasu's ingenious encoded translations utilise lower-case, capitalised, and small-caps fonts to show how Yi Sang inverted customs around the use of different Japanese scripts for foreign and native words, an underlying formal conceit that was also an act of protest.

At other times, the rhythm of the writing takes on a shifting, serial quality akin to Gertrude Stein or the Japanese modernist Kitasono Katué, whose 1959 minimalist opus 'Monotonous Space' – 'white square/ within it/ white square/ within it ...' is pre-empted by the opening lines of 'Au Magasin de Nouveautes': 'The square in the square in the square in the square in the square...' Here and elsewhere, Yi Sang's writing seems proleptically 'concrete' in the 1950s–60s sense, particularly where the tone of pseudo-scientific or rational enquiry is complemented by the use of abstract visual symbols.

In other places, the construction of byzantine logical systems that collapse in on themselves or become stretched to the point of incoherence, is reminiscent of Beckett's *Watt*:

> I climb up above the first floor to
> the second floor to the third floor
> to the rooftop garden and look
> to the south and there is nothing
> there and look to the north and
> there is nothing there and so I go
> down from the rooftop garden to
> the third floor to the second floor
> to the first floor and the sun that
> rose in the east has set in the west
> rose from the east and set in the
> west and rose from the east and set
> in the west ('Movement')

The poems that Yi Sang began publishing in Korean from 1933 – again, the choice of language was itself an act of resistance – perhaps express a closer connection between language and emotional or bodily impulse. Certainly, in Jack Jung's translations they are marked by a blooming of the subconscious, brilliant fragments of prose poetry enacting the performative causality of dreams:

> This ground was once the bottom of a primal lake. Salty. The pillars holding back
> the curtains become damp. Clouds do not come near me. My tonsils swell in the
> humorless air. There is a currency scandal—my hand, looking like a foot, shame–
> lessly holds the crone's throbbing hand.
>
> A rumor goes around about a tyrant's infiltration. Babies constantly turn into lit–
> tle grave mounds. The grown-ups' shoes hit other grown-ups' shoes. I never want
> to see them again, but where can I escape to? In a state of emergency, quaran–
> tined neighbors mingle. The distant cannon blasts and the blisters on our skins
> soothe us ('Street Outside Street')

Recurrent motifs – bodies, limbs (severed and prosthetic), mirrors, blood, ink, families and trees – come to comprise a sort of Surrealist mythopoesis, a fractured optic on contemporary political events (Jung's timeline informs us that 'Street Outside Street' is amongst a number of works making reference to the Japanese invasion of Manchuria). Also pressed into this symbology are anxieties around inheritance, patriarchy, sickness, and unrequited or scorned love.

The stories and essays, notwithstanding their own merits, add colour to the biographical details which frame Yi Sang's poetry. 'After Sickbed', a third-person biographical narrative, evokes the half-dreaming state in which he spent much time while receiving treatment for the tuberculosis that would kill him at the age of twenty-seven: 'His fever rose higher and higher into the night, and he lost consciousness, traveling between dream and reality'. 'Spider&Spider-MeetPigs' is a story of Kafkaesque abjection involving two anthropomorphic spiders, a fairy tale of imperial bondage.

Don Mee Choi's team of translators – those named above and Joyelle MacSweeney, whose moving poetic afterword deserves mention – has done a brilliant job in making a highly significant corpus of modernist poetry and prose available to an English-speaking audience.

The Visible We Love

Runaway, Jorie Graham (Carcanet)
Reviewed by Maitreyabandhu

In *The Master and His Emissary* – for my money the most important book on imagination and culture since George Steiner's *Real Presences* – Iain McGilchrist writes that one of the dangers of modernity is the 'willingness to accept an explicit manifesto or message ... as a substitute for imaginative experience'. Jorie Graham's *Runaway* could be read as an essay on this danger. The power of the book, and of her best work in general, comes from the conflict created between the instinct to make statements and the contrary pull of the imagination.

Graham's poetry is characterised by intensity, by an urgency of feeling and expression shading at times into desperation. Her best poems gather pressure as they go, like something being squeezed into the top of an airtight box. An important element of this pressure is her relationship with the great poetry of the past. Her yearning for lyric beauty founded on the natural world – derived from the Romantics, especially Keats – is in tension with her conviction that futurity makes such yearning obsolete.

Poetry is usually past-haunted, Graham's poetry is future-haunted. *Runaway* portrays our present as a dehumanised future of global warming, wild fires, species collapse, mass migration, information glut, surveillance technology, and AI. It is a wired-in, post-human world: 'here's where free choice vanished, here rights, here the / real meaning of the word'('Exchange'). The unique individual with her lyric voice has been deleted: 'My soul has its alarm tuned off' ('Overheard in the Herd'); 'My self, my one *one-self* isn't working for me' ('From the Transience'). Again and again, Graham privileges explicit message over 'imaginative experience', as if the urgency of our situation demands it.

> Must I put down
> here that this is long ago. That the
> sky has been invisible for years
> now. That the ash
> of our fires has covered the sun.
> That the fruit is stunted yellow
> mold when it appears
> at all and we have no produce to
> speak of. ('Tree')

On one hand the poems of *Runaway* are anti-lyrics. The daunting, almost suffocating, form of many of the poems – long, four-line blocks that run down the page like bars or planks – close off access to lyric flexibility. The language, under pressure, is forced into abstraction, sentences are truncated – if a poet's work could be illustrated by their characteristic punctuation, Auden's would be represented by the semicolon, Graham's by the full stop – or made to run together without punctuation, or mangled into textspeak: 'sd', 'yr', 'u'.

And yet, pulling in the opposite direction, is her lyric sensibility. Against the nightmare endgame of 'Tree', we hear echoes of Keats's Odes, especially 'To Autumn'. Graham's use of 'eglantine' harks back to 'Ode to a Nightingale'. Its 'beechen green, and shadows numberless' work against the wild fires:

> the twisting
> branches and multifaceted
> changing shades,
> and greens, and shades of greens,
> lobed, and lashing sun, the fig
> that seemed to me the
> perfect one, the ready one, it is
> permitted ('Tree')

Keats's bird, emblem of the lyric imagination, sings, perhaps for the last time, in poem after poem of *Runaway*: 'the wren has alighted right here camouflaged in normalcy' ('When Overfull of Pain I'). 'The blackbird in the thicket understands me I think' ('It Cannot Be'). 'A starling's wing /cld be my shadow on/ the monitor' ('The Nest®'). 'A crow lands on the tree. He tries to land. He/ settles, claws, but the grip slips, he rises then comes at it again' ('Sam's Standing').

The lyric impulse to speak to and for the natural world – the poet's soul talking directly to the soul of any or every reader – keeps tugging against the robotic sterility, without depth or memory, that wants to dominate this collection: 'I was human. I would have liked to speak of / that. But not now' ('[To] the Last [Be] Human'). In the same way, lyric elegy – 'There was the wasted splendour of day every day'– works against a Beckettian 'Nothing in all the directions' ('Becoming Other').

The best poems of *Runaway* are deadlocked between the need to make explicit and speak out, and the yearning to celebrate the implicit values of imagination: to touch and sing, to say 'fig' and 'robin'. A child starts to walk or to repeat a word. Birds cry at dawn. All the 'visible we love' wants to be cherished and elegised. 'I look at this foreign country, which was so ready, / which fell ill so suddenly'('When Overfull of Pain I').

Then there's the wind blowing through almost every poem. It might be Shelley's West Wind that might 'Scatter, as from an unextinguish'd hearth / Ashes and sparks, my words among mankind!' or the harbinger of a new barrenness. Occasionally, it is nature, in lyric dress, sighing for a lost world: 'here is an old wind, watch it orchestrate event' ('Overheard in the Herd'). 'After the high winds stop you're forced to hear / the freshness of what's / there' ('Scarcely There').

Graham's poetry is an urgent reminder of the crisis we face. It is also a plea – late and failing – for imaginative identification and for poetry's capacity (never entirely disavowed) to unite the self's depths with the beauty of the world.

Salt, flame

Where Now Begins, **Kerry Hardie (Bloodaxe Books) £9.95**
Reviewed by Sue Leigh

Kerry Hardie writes with clarity and directness of a world seen freshly. She can conjure a scene in a few words: a garden, a room, the landscape beyond her window. I admire the subtle way she moves towards insight. Her poems are deeply personal yet have a mythic quality.

Hardie lives in County Kilkenny with her husband, the writer Sean Hardie. (It is relevant to mention this as one has a sense of two lives lived alongside each other. 'This is the room we inhabit, / fragile as glass, / the light passing through' she writes in 'Real Estate'.) She describes this collection, her eighth, as a 'fairly dark book'. Written before the events of 2020, it reflects on time passing, conflict ('Civil War Aftermath' stands out), memory, relationships, ageing and the death of friends and family. But all this is weighed against an intense love for the physical world.

In 'Time Passing', my favourite poem in the book, Hardie longs to experience again a 'fierce lust for the world / but that's memory now'. Her love for the world has not diminished, and she looks for words that 'lie about in the piles of old rags / on the cluttered floor of my mind, / yet still the sweetness is here'. An elegy for her sister considers the bittersweet nature of life and love, 'salt, flame, / sweet honeycomb. / That is why we suffer so.' There are other elegies – for the poet Ciaran Carson, for friends; the loss of her father and the more recent death of her mother haunt many of the poems but she acknowledges that there is a time to move on, 'to lift down the coat / that has hung on the back of your door through the year. / The smell of the wearer has finally faded, / you can't pretend any more'. And in the end she starkly admits, 'You will also be dead ... the spirit moving to light, / the flesh settling into the clay'.

Poems about other relationships include 'Talking to My Stepson' in which there is regret: 'the past is a bath filled with water, long cooled' and 'what's done stays done forever'. In 'Bolt the Shutter' (with echoes of Yeats's 'Why Should Not Old Men Be Mad') the poet considers her ancestors: 'Where shall we go, they are saying, / when the hearth of your flesh grows cold? / Bare hills look out in answer, / and the clean empty skies of the morning'.

'Day Lilies' (a plant in which each flower lives for a day, making room for the next one lower down the stem) might be a metaphor for the way we have to live. 'So much I've been given and planted / in the wrong soil or at the wrong time', she writes, but she celebrates these gifts, relishing how they make the garden 'disordered, unruly and joyous'. In another poem about gardening, 'Hymn', she realises the futility of trying to control the garden after summer rain, the wisdom of letting things be, 'all that wild sappy life growing stronger and fiercer'.

The cycle of the seasons turns through the book. The poet is aware of that cycle beginning to close in for her too. In 'Crow-light' she watches the birds at the end of the year, when 'the sky was old and smoky with dusk'. She sees the birds in spring, summer and then again in 'Winter strong, and the land not caring, / and the slouch of fox, / and the white corpse staring.' To face that is to embrace life itself.

Up the Line to England

Vapour Trails: Reviews and Essays on Poetry, John Greening (Shoestring) £12.50
Reviewed by Martin Caseley

'I believe there is still such a thing as English poetry', regular *PN Review* contributor Greening states in his preface: the first half of this book accordingly explores 'Varieties of Englishness', as the subheading puts it. Beginning with the First World War poets Edward Thomas and Edmund Blunden, Greening surveys evidence for the survival of what might be lazily tagged 'traditional' English poetry. The ambiguities in Thomas's life and writing once again surface, whilst a brief examination of Blunden's work concludes 'he is not a complacent pastoralist; he is terrifying'. The former's apparent rural simplicity has long been challenged; the latter's work awaits similar recuperation. Greening finds, however, continuities in unusual places: Kathleen Raine, Norman Nicholson, Patricia Beer.

With the poetry of Raine, Greening considers whether her oracular mysticism is naive or 'compelling', concluding that avoidance of metaphor and the use of symbols allows writing that is somehow 'authentic' and archetypal. This deliberate narrowing of scope allows her to avoid abstraction, but one wonders if summarising her work as 'drawing-room civility' really has much purchase today. The case of Norman Nicholson is more straightforward, if puzzling. Like Charles Causley, another poet Greening is sympathetic to, he has been docketed as a regional writer, yet the fall of this former Faber author into obscurity has been swift. Greening concludes that his late work may prove more compelling than his rather formally old-fashioned celebrations of Millom and district. Regarding Patricia Beer, instead of focusing on locality, Greening isolates her 'understated' swerving style of tackling family, religion and death, making intriguing comparisons with Sharon Olds and Stevie Smith.

Several of these discussions isolate the traditions of an 'English line' – the lure of regionalism, old-fashioned tastes, religion, family trauma – but Greening balances the positives with care, reminding us that Patricia Beer as a reviewer possessed 'knife-skills' and that 'innocence' marked the early poems of Nicholson, just as it did Heaney's more celebrated work. He also explores curious byways (his nuanced discussion of Peter Redgrove's career is a case in point), but can seem a little indecisive when faced with a poet of the stature of Thom Gunn. Summarised in Clive Wilmer's words as 'not quite English', the discussion of his late work seems confused: it is surely highly debatable that he 'would prove to be a much better elegist than celebrant of the gay community', and there is much more to be said about *The Man with Night Sweats*, not least that beneath Gunn's 'cool, attentive' tone, deep wells of emotion prevail.

The final essay in this section of the book alights upon Simon Armitage, who would seem a poet designed to illustrate or refute notions of Englishness, but the discussion feels truncated and cursory. It is notable that, while finding room to discuss Carol Rumens, Helen Dunmore and Moniza Alvi, there is nothing on Carol Ann Duffy.

The accompanying essays on Irish and American poets provide a necessary counterpoint to all the Englishness, including thoughtful investigations of other miscellaneous names. A good case is made for the longer visionary work of Andrew Young, whilst the celebratory, but by no means uncritical, discussion of Eavan Boland left me wanting more. Additionally, the pieces on Berryman and Lowell are well-judged reassessments: Greening is surely right that Lowell's *Notebook*-period exhibits 'bleak, dead-end determination', rather than the exciting breakthroughs in *Life Studies*. Ideas of the persistence of Englishness have dissipated a little by the end of this book, but Greening's clear and judicious approach has much to recommend it.

Showing What's Noticed: Three Chapbooks

The Years, **Jamie McKendrick (Arc Publications) £8**
Archway Sonnets, **Kate Bingham (New Walk Editions) £5**
Fighters, Losers, **Declan Ryan (New Walk Editions) £5**
Reviewed by Paul McLoughlin

The Years opens with a pair of unrhymed sonnets, the second of which sets out with a fine addition to my cache of favourite line breaks: 'A life of doing nothing is a life / well-lived' (which is almost as good as Bernard O'Donoghue's 'These days what fills me with the greatest / Sense of achievement is getting out / Of doing things', from another poem on ageing). McKendrick's poem is called 'Doing Nothing', a reversal of the opening 'Nothing Doing' in which a heron gazes with 'sheer disgust' at the water in a pool 'left undrained to shiver through the winter' where 'nothing moves that's worth a sprat'. In the sestet, the poet-speaker, whose 'quiff quivers' and whose 'beak / is sharp as a tack' shows that he not only empathises with but has become the heron. The turn gives us access to this metamorphosis: 'I know the feeling ... The world is a con'. This is a poet enjoying himself, his cleverness a delight, as is that of John Fuller, to whom O'Donoghue's poem, 'Getting Out', is dedicated.

The 'thurn-harrier' in the hybrid sonnet-villanelle of that name is a 'bailiff beetle' that earns its 'hire' evicting a mythical-fictitious creature (the thurn) by harrying it from its home. Once again the anthropomorphic-personification palimpsest is evident when the thurn stuffs 'pamphlets in his case', including, perhaps, the one we are reading. Perhaps again, 'The Lion-Tree', issuing from a mention in Pliny the Elder and looking nothing like a lion, is extinct because it grew 'tired of its existence'; a suicidal tree that leads us to Granada's 'Court of the Lions', whose complex, paradisal water system might contrast with the opening poem's pool but instead contrasts two visits by the poet-speaker, fifty years apart, in a short, evocative poem whose final line has his older heart vibrate 'to the murmur of marble, the patter of water', a reference to Ibn Zamrak's poem carved round the courtyard's basin.

By the time we reach the final poem's 'untranslated last line of *Paradiso*' we can consider ourselves widely travelled, in Europe at least, after a journey aided by myth (the Mersey's foghorns lead out to 'Neptune's harsh bassoon' while a courtyard in Milan is filled with 'Cerberus barking'), and humour ('Nero still playing Bach on his violin'), history (the same poem's 'scattered city rising from its ruins') and memory ('I can see them all, as if they'd just / gathered in red and grey for morning roll call'). All the recto single-page poems are accompanied by McKendrick's accomplished verso artwork. The pictures offer an intriguing visual commentary on the poems but may equally be regarded quite separately, something McKendrick approves of.

Bingham's 'Archway Sonnets' includes a poem about talking to a puddle (the second of a trio that started life as a three-part single poem), and there are others on clothes in a washing machine, fly-tipped debris, and dinner plates left on a wall ('cheap willow-pattern rip-offs left to take'). They are the stuff of comfortable life in desirable London postcodes. But what poems they make. Bingham's rhythmic ear is impeccable and she is so good with rhyme the reader stops to admire it. This is a chapbook of sonnets all written in the same form (abcd x 3, plus closing couplet) which, if not original, is deftly deployed. These are poems that tell of the mundane. I could delve for treasures (they are easily found) but better, I think, to quote one sonnet in full:

Taller again this year, the garden roses
no one seems to remember planting loom
like neighbours, five or six feet over the pavement,
yellows, reds and pinks at human height,

nodding and beaming as I come and go,
each cluster's colour doubled in the gloom
of unlit living-room windows, each well-meant
intrusion twice as curious and bright.

All I have to do is show I notice
their magnificent nosey blousy blooms
for every flower to release its scent,
as if a rose could put the world to rights,

its tint illuminate June's moody weather,
its unfolding head keep mine together.

This is perfect, isn't it? Octave and sestet, a sentence each. And the conclusion's acceptance that looking and admiring do not in themselves put things right has something of Larkin's 'Love Songs in Age' about it, in meaning, syntax and tone.

It's a long way from an Archway postcode to the world of Declan Ryan's 'Fighters, Losers', a chapbook homage to American prize fighters. It opens and closes with poems about the lesser-known figures Diego 'Chico' Corrales and Jonathan Rendell. 'The Resurrection' shows us Corrales 'being borne aloft by his trainer and his cutman, / his arms stretched out crosswise, / celebrating coming back from the dead'. That Rendell 'boxed well enough to write about it' we learn from the poem that bears his name, and is attested to by one of the chapbook's epigraphs: 'I prefer losers. They're more self-aware'. We meet the expected Clay (and Ali), Marciano, Louis, Liston and Tyson but we do so in Lawrentian lines not to be found in sports pages; and Ryan is interested in more than physical pain. When Tyson is knocked out in an adoring Japan by the no-hoper Buster Douglas, whom he had floored earlier in the fight, 'Tyson will say / "I just stopped caring. / He got up. Nobody else had"'. Corrales dies:

on the Fort Apache Road in Las Vegas,
his Suzuki motorcycle in component parts,
his license expired, his blood three times the legal alcohol limit.
'Bottom line, no one else did anything wrong',
Sergeant Tracy McDonald will say,
following a report. 'He basically killed himself.'

Which is what the civilised world will always say. It's become a brave subject. Those of us who bought *The Ring* and avidly pored over its numbered lists of contenders are in grave danger of being cancelled. The ostensibly looser, discursive lines of Ryan's poems contrast with the more formal (though equally leisurely) compactness of McKendrick's and with the uniform delicacy of Bingham's sonnets, but all three poets are writing about what they notice and what they find themselves interested in, which is what poets do at their reliable best. The chapbooks are also a testament to the smaller publishing outlets they issue from.

Momently Carried Across

Mad John's Walk, John Gallas (Five Leaves); *The King of the Lam*, Greg Delanty (Southword Editions); *Satyress*, Audrey Molloy (Southword Editions); *Parturition*, Heather Treseler (Southword Editions)
Reviewed by Rory Waterman

Every couple of months, my beneficent masters at *PNR* Acres dispatch a big Jiffy bag full of pamphlets to me, and I leaf through them idly, between a cafetière and a recycling bin. A fair proportion are always evidently either plausible or good, so I sort those quite hastily into a 'maybe' pile and then spend too much of my time anxiously determining which deserve my column inches. But there is a third category, less common to *books* of poems, and overlapping the other two. Let us label it 'fascinatingly odd'. When I come across some of the pamphlets in this misshapen group, I am reminded of the origins of the pamphlet or 'chapbook' in street literature, broadside ballads and unfashionable and unsanctioned political and personal outpourings, and sometimes I get really excited.

John Gallas's *Mad John's Walk* just about fits into this category, and comes from the press of Five Leaves Bookshop in Nottingham, which has a proudly radical political outlook and, by some estimations, the best poetry selection in the UK outside London. To introduce it, I may as well emulate the practice of some poetry reviewers at our only newspapers that still carry poetry reviews, and lean on the blurb – though I'll quote rather than paraphrase: 'In the autumn of 2016, poet John Gallas decided to follow the route taken by John Clare when he escaped from Matthew Allen's High Beach Asylum in Epping Forest and made his way back to his home in Northborough. This pamphlet is a light-hearted account of that eighty-mile journey'. Gallas is habitually witty and warm, and indeed the pamphlet is as irreverent as one would expect. It begins with a poem in which he writes that:

I threw myself into a stubbled field
with half an apple and the Book of Clare
to read a store of verslings midst the bees ...
        The hay
stood stacked in stooks, and down the half-flowered twitch
the planted pylons strod. So I began.

If this were just a silly pamphlet, though, there would be little to recommend it. What follows is an eight-page prose diary, really a diarised travel memoir-essay, as limpid as it is intellectually sprightly, interspersed with snippets of Clare's poems, and tinged with elegiac sadness and self-deprecation, for all of its smiles. He knows there is no following in Clare's footsteps, really: 'I took a spare T-shirt, a spare pair of socks, a rollable raincoat, a hat, the Penguin *Clare*, a notebook and pen, and my iPod Fitness app, to measure each damned step along the way. John C. had old boots, and nothing else'. But the pamphlet's glory is in the parallels as well as the divergences, and Gallas's occasional cool insights: 'If madness was missing, I felt still that I held his hand all the way, but that we did not talk about life. Sometimes, that is Poetry'. Or: 'At Stevenage, I hurried through'. (Always wise.) 'Leaving the town, on a hot, wide pavement, I saw a small orange lying in my way. I looked at it. What, I asked myself, would John Clare do? Naturally, I ate it'.

There isn't much here for the National Rambler's Association to purloin for marketing purposes: 'I hurried down the main road into town, facing the terrible onslaught of rush hour. I leapt from tussock to weed along the roadside as cars driven with furious intent lifted my bag off my back each second in their slipstream. I longed for 1841'. (There are brief exceptions, such as when he pauses in a 'Paradise' where 'poppies and birdsong wibbled on all sides' and determines 'to eat grass'.) But this pamphlet is as likely to inspire the imagination as it is unlikely to inspire wanderlust in the English countryside. The pamphlet ends with five very short poems, one for each day of the journey, wryly echoing the formal, thematic and linguistic properties of its inspiration:

The wheat stands up, unbowed and new.
The church stands up behind.
I am the less contented kind,
For all that God can do.

It has its purpose and its law,
And God has his Career;
While I am left to wander here
And wonder what I'm for.

I wish Gallas had thought to find a way to avoid both unnecessary uses of 'up', but taken as a whole this little poem encapsulates the tones of the pamphlet. It would be easy to have too much of this sort of thing, but Gallas keeps things brief, and I am confident that readers will come away thinking they have spent a good half hour with the Mad Johns.

Southward Editions, the publishing arm of Munster Literature Centre, has recently got into the habit of publishing several pamphlets a year, and in 2020 has given birth to impressive triplets, including Greg Delanty's *The King of the Lam*, a moving and often calmly removed set of elegies for the Irish-language poet Liam Ó Muirthile: 'We never finished our on-hold confabulation'. I'd also like to give a nod of appreciation to Audrey Molloy's *Satyress*, which is as sassy as its title implies. The prose poem 'A Brief History of Smoking' is a crisp nostalgic elegy, and an elegy for a time of nostalgia: 'On the nightstand, like a carriage clock, Dunhill's claret-and-gold pack; alas, now gone, replaced with images that would put you off coming.' She can also be more tersely and gently poignant, as in the exquisite 'Envy Is a Daylily', which ends: 'someone / once looked upon your life / wishing it were theirs'.

My pick of the three, though, is *Parturition* by the American Heather Treseler, who (like Molloy) is yet to publish a full collection. Treseler has a predilection for writing multi-page poems in long-lined, heavily enjambed couplets. She could clearly be a superbly inquisitive personal memoirist, but has for now decided to formulate her ideas into poems and has found a fitting verse form for them – though some of her enjambments ('Fabergé / Egg') feel like the product of an automatic line-cutting machine rather than poetic necessity. Most of these engrossing poems quantum leap around an anecdote, often regarding someone the poet apparently knows. The opener, 'Louisiana Requiem', begins: 'Eight months pregnant when your mother began hospice, / you sat in the driveway'. In order to give a flavour of her insistent style, it is necessary to quote at length, and this is from the poem's ensuing meditation, which is typically dense but rewards the careful thought it demands:

> And you are an entire country,
> an America, stretched impossibly across a Mason Dixon
>
> And two shores, nearing: the
> woman who bore you, daughter
> You will bear, your body a hinge
> between its history
>
> and future, an imperfect present
> tense. Scientist, dedicated
> to cool notice of detailed fact,
> resistant to the muddled
>
> logic of metaphor, you nonetheless find yourself borne
> across by likeness in otherwise
> radical difference:
>
> the shared violence that marks
> birth and death, mothering
> the grade that governs the
> latitudes of the in-between.

A common method of Treseler's is to wrap her poem's anecdotes in the experiences of someone else, so that we have one impression seen through another. Thus, in 'Skywalker':

> Years after recovery, you encounter a sinewy woman
> in a Lacan seminar who can't
> shut up about desire,
>
> drive, deferral, her eloquence a
> kind of death-flirting
> performance like Charles
> Blondin tightroping
>
> across Niagara in a blindfold.

Occasionally, she is more direct, but the poems are never less scrupulous – or vulnerable: 'For you, I have left my clothes on the floor', and am 'open to rapture or / metaphor: a chance to be momently carried across'.

Contributors

Yeow Kai Chai is a poet, fiction writer, and editor. He has three poetry collections, *One to the Dark Tower Comes* (2020), *Pretend I'm Not Here* (2006) and *Secret Manta* (2001). **Thomas McCarthy** was born in County Waterford, Ireland, in 1954. He worked at Cork City Library for many years. Carcanet published his most recent collection, *Prophecy*, in 2019. His *Pandemonium* (Carcanet, 2016) was short-listed for the *Irish Times*/Poetry Now Award. **John FitzGerald**'s first full-length collection will appear from Gallery Press in June 2021. A chapbook *First Cut* was published by Southward Editions in 2017. He won the Patrick Kavanagh Award in 2014. **Jeffrey Kahrs** lived in Istanbul for eighteen years. He won the Nazim Hikmet Poetry Contest and edited several publications about Turkish poetry. He appeared in *Talisman*, *What Rough Beast* and *The Bosphorus Review of Books*, among others. **Anthony Barnett**'s new book, with drawings by Lucy Rose Cunningham, is *Book Paradise: Spillikins.* He publishes the review *Snow lit rev.* **Caroline Clark**'s first collection is *Saying Yes in Russian* (Agenda, 2012); her second, *Sovetica,* is forthcoming from CB Editions. **Peter Scupha**m, at 88, is one of our oldest, if not most venerable, poets. He appeared in the very first *PNR* and has never quite disappeared. He is safely locked down, or up, in an Elizabethan Norfolk house nearly as old as he is. **Tony Roberts**'s fifth collection, *The Noir American & Other Poems*, was published in 2018. His second book of essays on poets, critics and America, *The Taste of My Mornings*, appeared in 2019. Both are from Shoestring Press. **Reem Abbas** is a writer of poetry and occasional prose. She is also a doctoral candidate at the University of Cambridge and is currently working on Basil Bunting's Persian literary and artistic influences. **Jane Duran** has published five collections of her poetry with Enitharmon Press. Her forthcoming book *the clarity of distant things* is due from Carcanet in the autumn. **Helena Nelson** runs Happen*Stance* Press and sphinxreview.co.uk. She also sometimes writes poems. **Horatio Morpurgo** is an environmental campaigner, essayist and poet. *Lady Chatterley's Defendant & Other Awkward Customers* was published by Just Press in 2011; *The Paradoxal Compass* by Notting Hill Editions in 2017. During the 1992–95 war in the former Yugoslavia, **Michael Brett** worked in the Information Centre of BosniaHerzegovina in London. He was runner up in the Isle of Skye Iolaire Arts Foundation Poetry Prize, and twice runner up for the Bridport Prize. **Francis O'Hare** was born in Newry, NI, in 1970. He has published several collections in Ireland and the US, his most recent being *Sailing to Omeath*, with Arlen House, Dublin. **Martin Caseley** lives in Norfolk and his essays, articles and poems appear regularly in *PN Review, Agenda* and *The Countryman.* He also reviews books and music for the *international times* website, and has recently written about Clive James, Bob Dylan, Geoffrey Hill, Ronnie Lane and Jeremy Hooker. **Marius Kociejowski** is a poet, essayist and travel writer. Carcanet published his *God's Zoo: Artists, Exiles, Londoners* (2014) and *Collected Poems* (2019). Forthcoming (Autumn, 2021): *A Factotum in the Book Trade* (Biblioasis). **Shane McCrae**'s most recent book is *Sometimes I Never Suffered* (Corsair, 2020), which was shortlisted for the T.S. Eliot Prize. He lives in New York City. **Maurice Riordan**'s fifth collection from Faber & Faber, *The Shoulder Tap*, will be published in October.

Colophon

Editors
Michael Schmidt
John McAuliffe

Editorial Manager
Andrew Latimer

Contributing Editors
Vahni Capildeo
Sasha Dugdale
Will Harris

Design
Cover and Layout
Emily Benton Book Design

Typesetting
Andrew Latimer

Editorial address
The Editors at the address on the right. Manuscripts cannot be returned unless accompanied by a stamped addressed envelope or international reply coupon.

Trade distributors
NBN International

Represented by
Compass IPS Ltd

ISBN 978-1-7841-083-7-3
ISSN 0144-7076

Subscriptions—6 issues
INDIVIDUAL–print and digital: £39.50; abroad £49
INSTITUTIONS–print only: £76; abroad £90
INSTITUTIONS–digital only: from Exact Editions (https://shop.exacteditions.com/gb/pn-review) to: PN Review, Alliance House, 30 Cross Street, Manchester, M2 7AQ, UK.

Supported by

Supported using public funding by ARTS COUNCIL ENGLAND